A STAR DANCED

A Star Danced is a sumptuously designed celebration of Audrey Hepburn's life, containing 150 superb photographs. It tells the story of her life, from her childhood in Nazi-occupied Holland, through her early aspirations to become a ballet dancer, her début on screen to instant and universal acclaim and her years as one of Hollywood's most sought-after stars, to her later life working among the poorest children of the Third World.

After a series of minor revue and film roles in London, Hepburn was spotted by Colette, who immediately cast her in the central role of a Broadway adaptation of her last novel, *Gigi.* Soon afterwards she was offered a role alongside Gregory Peck in *Roman Holiday,* for which she collected the Best Actress Oscar. More successful parts followed: she won the Tony Award for Best Actress for *Ondine,* captivated audiences as Natasha in *War and Peace,* and was highly praised for her brilliance in a serious role in *The Nun's Story.*

Hepburn's dress sense was close to perfection and her clothes — many of them by Givenchy, who dressed her for *Funny Face* in 1957 — placed her on the world's twelve Best Dressed Women list for several years. Her personality and sensuous yet untouchable beauty made her irresistible to the public. On Hepburn's death, Liz Taylor said, 'God has a most beautiful new angel now, that will know just what to do in heaven.'

Robyn Karney's work in film includes writing and editing, film criticism and film story consultancy. She is the editor of *Who's Who in Hollywood* and the co-author with Ronald Bergan of Bloomsbury's highly acclaimed *Foreign Film Guide.*

*. . . but then there was a star danced,
and under that was I born.*

MUCH ADO ABOUT NOTHING ACT II, SCENE 1

AUDREY HEPBURN

A STAR DANCED

ROBYN KARNEY

ARCADE PUBLISHING · NEW YORK

FIRST U.S. EDITION 1995

First published in the United Kingdom by Bloomsbury Publishing

PICTURE SOURCES

Advertising Archives: pages 45, 165
Aquarius: pages 27, 51, 56, 69, 82 *top*, 87 *bottom*, 98, 118, 134, 138 *left*, 148, 155, 156, 163, 169, 171, 182, 183
Richard Avedon, Inc., New York: pages 8–9
Camera Press: page 140 *bottom*
Camera Press/Cecil Beaton: page 11
Camera Press/Henry Gris: page 167
Camera Press/Terry O'Neill: pages 151, 152, 153, 154, 157
Camera Press/Norman Parkinson: page 10
Eileen Darby: pages 42, 45
E.T. Archive: page 14
Joel Finler: pages 64, 70 *top*, 132 *bottom*, 133 *top*, 138 *right*
Gamma/Frank Spooner Pictures: pages 13, 166, 177, 180, 184, 185
Ronald Grant Collection: pages 32, 36 *top*, 37, 38 *bottom*, 40, 70 *bottom*, 71, 78, 79, 87 *top*, 99, 112, 114, 131, 139, 161
Hulton Deutsch Collection: pages 29, 73, 174
Katz Pictures/Peter Charlesworth: pages 181, 192
Kobal Collection: pages 38 *top*, 41, 46, 54, 56, 68, 74, 76, 77, 80, 81, 82 *bottom*, 84, 85, 86, 90, 94, 101, 115, 120, 121, 132 *top*, 133 *bottom*, 176
Moviestore Collection: pages 89, 97, 160, 172–3
New York Public Library: page 63
Popperfoto: pages 12, 20, 21, 25, 31, 36 *bottom*, 49, 117, 164
Rex Features: pages 22, 24, 26, 52, 158, 159, 179
Tiffany and Co.: page 187
Warner Brothers Pictures Inc.: pages 95–6
Bob Willoughby: pages 53, 102–10, 122–130, 136–7, 140 *top*, 141–6

Grateful acknowledgment is made to Hodder and Stoughton Limited for permission to quote from *Audrey* by Charles Higham (New English Library), and to Ian Woodward, Rupert Crew Limited and Virgin for permission to quote from *Audrey Hepburn: Fair Lady of the Screen*, copyright © 1984, 1993 by Ian Woodward.

ISBN 1-55970-300-8
Library of Congress Catalog Card Number 94-79751
Library of Congress Cataloging-in-Publication information is available.

Published in the United States by Arcade Publishing, Inc., New York
Distributed by Little, Brown and Company

10 9 8 7 6 5 4 3 2 1

Designed by Bradbury and Williams

PRINTED IN SPAIN

For Helen Bourne

Author's Note and Acknowledgements

This book was commissioned by Bloomsbury while Audrey Hepburn was still alive. Alas, her tragic and premature death rendered an exciting project both sad and difficult, since it denied me access not only to the subject herself, but to many people for whom her death was too close.

None the less, I have tried to give as accurate an account as possible of her extraordinary life and qualities and have, at least, been able to view again the films which are her lasting testament.

I owe a debt of gratitude to several people. My researcher, David Oppedisano, attended to the unglamorous aspects of the work with his customary good humour; Bernard Hrusa-Marlow and Tom Vallance gave invaluable assistance in numerous ways, including making the films available to me. Clive Hirschhorn once again allowed me access to his library, and Tim Wilson in New York sent filmed and printed material.

A special thank you to Fred Zinnemann who generously gave of his time, and to John McCallum who wrote from Australia; to Andrew Thomas of the Avedon Studio in New York and to Avedon himself for the privilege of using his portrait. Marion Hume, fashion editor of the *Independent*, Tasha Hudson at Caroline Neville Associates (representing Hubert de Givenchy), Jane Pritchard at the Ballet Rambert and Terry Charman at the Imperial War Museum were very helpful, as were Sue Sharp who translated French interviews, Robin Cross, Angie Errigo, Trevor Willsmer, Patrick Palmer and Vivien Heilbron.

My copy editor, Delayne Aarons, dedicated herself to cleaning up the manuscript way beyond the call of duty, picture researcher Anne-Marie Ehrlich was a pleasure to work with, and my agent Tony Peake was a source of strength.

Special appreciation is due to David Reynolds at Bloomsbury for his encouragement, support and practical help, and to Penny Phillips.

Robyn Karney
London 1993

CONTENTS

INTRODUCTION

My own life has been much more than a fairy tale. I've had my share of difficult moments, but. . . whatever difficulties I've gone through, I've always gotten a prize at the end

AUDREY HEPBURN

I am, and forever will be, devastated by the gift of Audrey Hepburn before my camera. I cannot lift her to greater heights. She is already there. I can only record, I cannot interpret her. There is no going further than who she is. She has achieved in herself her ultimate portrait

RICHARD AVEDON

Like Margot Fonteyn, her counterpart in the world of ballet, Audrey Hepburn trailed a cloud of magic wherever she went, both on screen and off.

Hepburn – in the words of Rex Reed 'as rare as a blue giraffe' – was an original. There have been others more immediately and obviously beautiful, and many of superior acting ability; but her personality – a blend of frail girl and elegant woman, of wit, poetry, vulnerability and 'class' – was unique.

One of the most famous film stars in the world, she was certainly the best-loved (and earned astronomical fees equalled only by Elizabeth Taylor). Yet her film career came about more by accident than by design. Her progress from relative obscurity to first-time-out Academy Award-winner reads, fittingly for the girl dubbed 'the Princess' by Frank Sinatra, like a fairy tale.

The millions of extravagant words that have been written about her, and the interviews that she so reluctantly (but always graciously) gave, repeat the same salient facts, the same, sometimes contradictory, accounts she offered of her own beliefs and ambitions. The few details she chose to reveal about her past, particularly the war years, remained, however, consistent, differing only in a choice of words or the style of the journalist reporting them. She never wavered in her

Richard Avedon: Audrey Hepburn, 20 January 1967, New York.

professionalism and pursuit of excellence, in her self-denigration with regard to her gifts, and in her deeply-felt commitment to her marriages, her own children, and the children of a world ravaged by disasters.

It was Audrey Hepburn's unique achievement to become as renowned for her style as for her films, influencing the dress sense of a generation and beyond; to retain the loyalty of her audiences and her colleagues during long

Far left: A youthful Hepburn as seen by Norman Parkinson.

Left: The perfect hat face captured by Cecil Beaton . . .

. . . and, *above*, a fashion fantasy created by the same photographer.

absences from the screen; and to earn international respect for her selfless efforts as an ambassador for UNICEF – the last of the role she played to perfection on the public stage.

Hepburn's career followed a curious pattern. After a traumatic adolescence in Nazi-occupied Holland, she went to England to study ballet. Her height, and economic necessity, hindered her aspirations and led her into cabaret and films. In the course of thirty-eight years, she appeared in a modest total of twenty-six films.

The first half-dozen of these saw her in bit parts and small

Hepburn, aged twenty-four, receives the Best Actress Oscar for *Roman Holiday* from actor Jean Hersholt. Almost forty years later, in 1993, she became a (posthumous) recipient of the Jean Hersholt Humanitarian Award.

supporting roles, which brought her attention within the British film industry, but no public recognition. This came in 1953 with her American début film, *Roman Holiday*, for which, at the age of twenty-four, she collected the Best Actress Oscar.

The love affair with the world's press, valentines masquerading as reviews, was already well under way. Adoring cinemagoers everywhere waited impatiently for her next film. The Hollywood establishment, at once charmed and bemused, had never encountered anyone quite like her.

When Hepburn 'arrived' in Hollywood, seemingly from nowhere, there was an established order of female screen personalities, staple heroines who fell broadly into categories: the sex goddess, the *femme fatale*, the sex kitten, the girl next door, the sharp-tongued wisecracker, the screwball comedienne, the musical comedy star and the dignified dowager.

Such was Hollywood when she came on the scene. Into the bevy of blondes, beauties and bosoms, most of them all-American girls, from a variety of backgrounds across the country, intruded a waif: a thin, gangling, flat-chested child-woman, with irregular teeth, a wide jawbone, flaring nostrils and 'bat-wing' eyebrows. Her haircut was described by Cecil

Beaton as 'rat-nibbled', and she spoke with a curious cadence in an alluringly hybrid Anglo-European accent. Yet she carried herself with an ethereal grace and entranced with a smile at once wistful and radiant. Her eyes, her most remarkable feature, were large dark pools of expressiveness, registering every nuance of emotion – she would have been a consummate actress of the silent screen.

Audrey Hepburn's looks and personality broke the mould governing success on the American screen: as Billy Wilder famously put it, 'This girl, singlehanded, will make bust measurements a thing of the past.' Likewise, the conduct of her personal and professional life broke every rule. Characterised from the outset by reticence and modesty, class and style, warmth, humour and driven perfectionism, she became an instant icon.

Dressed on screen and off by Givenchy, with whom her image will always be identified, she was worshipped by fashion designers and photographers. Michael Kors said of her, 'Through the years, Audrey Hepburn has projected an image of style, not of fashion.' Isaac Mizrahi, attempting the largely hopeless task of describing her magic in words, said, 'Her sexiness sort of enters through

With Hubert de Givenchy, who shaped her fashion image and became a devoted friend.

your heart not through your groin. She appeals to the heart and spirit and head. She has to do with elevation and enlightenment.' She was endlessly and exquisitely photographed by the leading photographers of the day: Norman Parkinson, Cecil Beaton, Karsh of Ottawa, Anthony Armstrong-Jones and, of course, Avedon.

Grace, dignity, charm and compassion were Hepburn's hallmarks, along with total commitment to the task in hand. Kind, considerate and serious-minded, she also had a wonderful sense of humour which illuminated choice moments in her films, and was known as a great 'giggler'. Comedienne Lucille Ball said of her, 'She's a tomboy and a fine comedienne. You'd never think of her being able to do my type of comedy. But she can . . . But, well, she's so beautiful, so ethereal, it would be sacrilege to put her through it.'

The world's most famous gamine matured into a radiantly lovely and elegant woman, leaving a record of her sublime looks and personality in such loved films as *Sabrina, Funny Face, The Nun's Story, Breakfast at Tiffany's, Charade, My Fair Lady* and *Two for the Road.*

At the annual Academy Award ceremony in Hollywood on 29 April 1993, Audrey Hepburn was the joint recipient (with Elizabeth Taylor) of the Jean Hersholt Humanitarian Award. To the great sadness of all, she was no longer alive to receive it.

Presenting the Oscar statuette to Audrey's son Sean Hepburn Ferrer, her first leading man – and lifelong friend – Gregory Peck spoke for millions when he said,

'Throughout her career she was a symbol of grace and beauty, high style and high spirits, sophistication and sly innocence. To those of us who worked with her, she was a sensitive artist of beautiful colour.

'There was a part of her life that preoccupied her even more than her acting career. As a special ambassador for UNICEF, the United Nations Children's Fund, she tirelessly travelled the world, an advocate for the poor, the dispossessed, the starving – the people who never saw her radiance on screen and probably never would . . .

'The Jean Hersholt Humanitarian Award honours individuals in the motion picture industry whose humanitarian efforts have brought credit to us all. If *ever* someone lived up to the ideals of this award, with dedication and conviction, it was Audrey Hepburn.'

As one American journalist wrote, 'Audrey Hepburn fed our insatiable movie fantasies with exquisite finesse – rarely, if ever, letting us down. When she felt she had given enough, she began to live for herself, and in living for herself she gave hope and inspiration to others who knew nothing of her legend.'

This is the story of that legend, her life and her work.

WHO IS AUDREY, WHAT IS SHE...?

Huis Doorn, originally the property of the Van Heemstra family, and the last refuge of Kaiser Wilhelm II of Germany.

1

I was a very ordinary-looking little girl – thin, bony, straight-haired, bewildered

AUDREY HEPBURN

Audrey Hepburn fits none of the clichés and none of the clichés fits her

TIME MAGAZINE

Clues to Audrey Hepburn's originality are to be found in the background and events that shaped her. She was born on 4 May 1929, to parents who, in the words of writer Charles Higham, 'constituted a slightly indelicate pairing of the aristocracy and the bourgeoisie'. The baby daughter, christened Edda Kathleen Van Heemstra Hepburn-Ruston, was a 'long baby' with the 'prettiest laughing eyes'. From the outset, she was fragile, quiet and shy – 'a changeling in a family of sturdy charmers'.

The 'indelicate pairing' referred to by Higham was that of J.A. Hepburn-Ruston, a highly-placed Anglo-Irish banker, divorced and reportedly irresistible to women, and the Baroness Ella Van Heemstra, a Dutch aristocrat of distinguished lineage, divorced, the mother of two small sons, and still young and beautiful.

The Van Heemstras, a long line of wealthy, land-owning Dutch aristocrats, had close connections with the Royal household, which several of them had served in various capacities. The men distinguished themselves in the military, in government administration and in the law. They were proud, dutiful, honourable and cultivated people.

Audrey's mother was the third daughter of Baron Aarnoud Van Heemstra, a dignified and eminent lawyer who attended at the Court of Queen Wilhelmina. He had been, for a time, the Burgomaster of Arnhem, and was afterwards appointed to the governership of Dutch Guiana (later Suriname), which colony he ruled with distinction from 1921 to 1928.

In 1896, he had married Elbrig Van Asbeck, a baroness in her own right, whose antecedents could be traced to the twelfth century and included Hungarian, French and Jewish stock. Aarnoud and Elbrig had five daughters (one of whom became lady-in-waiting to Queen Juliana) and a son. This sizeable brood spent much of their childhood on one of the large family estates at Doorn in Utrecht, living in a splendid castle surrounded by a moat and several hundred acres of verdant countryside.

Today, Het Kasteel De Doorn, as the castle was known, is called simply Huis-Doorn, and is open to the public as a stately home-cum-museum. It figures in the history books as the last refuge of Kaiser Wilhelm II, who bought it from Baroness Elbrig Van Heemstra soon after his flight from Germany towards the end of World War I. At this time, 1918, the Van Heemstras had moved residence to another of their ancestral estates near Arnhem where, in 1920, their daughter Ella married the Honourable Jan Van Ufford, also a distinguished aristocrat and servant of the Royal household.

This was a stormy union, which ended in divorce five years and two sons later. Baroness Ella Van Heemstra, as she reverted to calling herself, and her boys, Alexander and Ian, spent periods of time with her parents in Suriname. There she met Joseph Hepburn-Ruston, who, as managing director of the Brussels branch of the Bank of England, was closely concerned with the administration of the Van Heemstras' financial affairs and properties.

The couple were married in Batavia (now Jakarta) in September 1926, and in due course took up residence outside Brussels. It was here, in a large, elegant and gracious nineteenth-century house, set in attractive grounds, that their first and only child was born. Despite the proverbial silver spoon in her mouth, she displayed neither the robust physicality that characterises the Dutch nor the confident, outgoing personality that went with her lineage.

Audrey Hepburn's later life bore, to a pronounced degree, all the marks of a childhood and adolescence that turned out to be a striking amalgam of privilege and deprivation. Inculcated with

Mother Ella and baby Audrey.

Little Audrey. No sign of the wraith-like beauty to come.

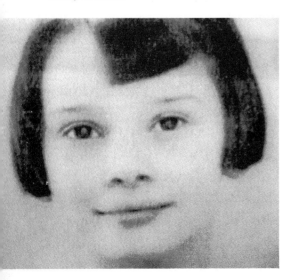

the breeding, culture, discipline and history of the Van Heemstras (whose portraits graced the walls of art galleries and museums as well as those of fine private houses), spending her early years in luxurious and idyllic surroundings, she wanted for nothing. She loved her half-brothers, in whose company she lost her shyness and played the tomboy with evident relish; her relationship with her mother was a close one, which she later admitted had the greatest influence on her. The attachment remained strong until Ella's death in 1984.

However, Baroness Van Heemstra was as formidable as she was admirable. She acted as the strong-willed guardian of her daughter's interests, and her disagreement over certain issues, notably the men in Audrey's life, made for periodic difficulties. Towards the end of her life, Audrey, who was always driven by the need for love and affection, spoke of her mother in an American television interview with Professor Richard Brown: 'It is true that I had an extraordinary mother. She herself was not a very affectionate person in the sense that I today consider affection. I spent a lot of time looking for it — and I found it. She was a *fabulous* mother but she came from an era — she was born in 1900, Victorian

influence still — of great discipline, of great ethics . . . a lot of love within her, not always able to show it. And *very* strict.'

When Ella Van Heemstra was growing up, her father held the traditional view that well-born young women avoided having any truck with the stage and the people connected with it. They were not considered respectable. The independent-minded Baroness no longer shared this opinion. Her authoritarian style of parenting notwithstanding, she encouraged her daughter's early enthusiasms for music and dance, and supported her later ambitions.

While still a tiny child, Audrey manifested a passionate love of animals, flowers and the countryside, which endured throughout her life. Other than enjoying games with her brothers, she was a solitary little girl, preferring to play with kittens, puppies and rabbits rather than other children. Reclusive and hypersensitive, she reacted badly to tensions and unhappiness, yet was capable of enjoyment, high spirits, and an impish and infectious sense of humour. A daydreamer who loved dressing up in her mother's clothes, she was keenly responsive to music and, as soon as she was able to read, became an avid bookworm, much influenced by her brother Ian.

Their shared enthusiasm for books was one of the few private memories that she articulated in detail in later years, telling the London *Evening News*, 'He's the original bookworm and when we were children he was devoted to Kipling. I admired him so much that I read all Kipling's books because I wanted to be like him . . . The result was that I had read nearly every book by Edgar Wallace and E. Phillips Oppenheim before I was 13. Those were real adventure books, and to me as a girl they had far more appeal than "Topsy Goes to School".'

This strong response to literature, combined with her refusal to play with dolls, which she considered 'silly', are early indications of the paradoxes that would come to characterise her image and persona in later years. The girl who hated dolls would grow to love children and long for her own; the taste for exciting thrillers and adventure stories was superseded by her devotion to fairy stories. She said, in the same interview, 'If I ever want to accentuate the importance of anything in any form of entertainment, it is the quality of the fairy tale . . . people go to the theatre and the cinema for the same reason that makes them like fairy tales – the sense of watching something that isn't real. The fairy tale is, to my mind, the core of entertainment.'

Early childhood, then, was protected and comfortable, a period of privileged play in wonderful surroundings, nurtured by nannies, governesses, and private tutors. Time was divided between the family estates in Belgium and Holland and, from the age of four, England, where she was taken during the winter months. But a shadow was cast over this seemingly perfect existence by tensions which arose in her parents' marriage. By all accounts, the major cause of strife between the Hepburn-Rustons was the husband's method of handling his wife's financial affairs. Conflict degenerated into open quarrel, creating an atmosphere that clearly distressed Audrey. During her father's frequent absences abroad on bank business, she seemed happy enough within the limitations of her grave and shy personality, but his homecomings upset the child. She would then withdraw into her shell, hiding in the nearby fields and, in a classic syndrome of misery, eating compulsively. Chocolates were a particular favourite and, despite her almost painful thinness throughout most of her life, she went through a period of ungainly puppy fat.

In 1935, when Audrey was six, without preamble or explanation, her father left the household never to return. He settled in London, where his upper-class social circle included Sir Oswald and Lady Diana Mosley and Hitler's girlfriend Unity Mitford. He forged ever closer links with these acquaintances, and became a wholehearted supporter of Mosley's Fascist movement, marching with the British Black Shirts. His daughter's views on this turn of events have not been made public. Apparently, when World War II was over he was living in Ireland, but there are conflicting accounts as to whether or not she ever saw him again after the outbreak of the war.

Meanwhile, and contrary to expectation, when her parents' divorce was finalised some considerable time after Hepburn-Ruston's exit, he insisted on regular access to his daughter. The practical outcome of the settlement was that Audrey, not yet ten, shy, jittery, self-consciously critical of her appearance and temperamentally unsuited to the rigours of a hearty, hockey-playing English educational establishment, was shipped off to an exclusive girls' boarding school near London. With the unyielding determination to put a positive gloss on a negative situation that coloured all her public comments, she confessed many years later that she had been 'terrified', but that 'it ended up being a good lesson in independence'.

In the event, Audrey's relatively brief sojourn at the school proved of profound significance to her future. The strict regime, academic demands and communal living for so reclusive a young girl must have been a shock to the system. She had been a sickly child and now developed the migraine headaches that would continue to plague her. But the difficulties of adjustment were quickly compensated for by the ballet lessons she began to take at the school. When Baroness Van Heemstra arrived to meet her daughter at the end of the first term, she found a new Audrey: lively, enthusiastic and obsessed with dance. From that moment on, ballet became her passion, Pavlova her heroine and stardom her aspiration.

London broadened her horizons in other directions. She was taken to the major historical monuments such as the Tower and learned about the queens who had perished there; she visited the National Gallery, enjoyed the Zoo at Regent's Park (nearby to where Ella rented an apartment),

experienced the thrills of Madame Tussaud's, and responded with enthusiasm to that uniquely British form of entertainment the Christmas pantomime.

The pattern of Audrey's life seemed set for several years to come when, on 3 September 1939, Britain declared war on Hitler's Germany. Baroness Van Heemstra, fearing a Nazi invasion of England, prevailed upon her ex-husband to send their daughter back to Holland in the interests of her safety – not just Holland, but Arnhem, a city close to the German border which would have to endure some of the severest consequences of the Occupation.

But the irony of Baroness Van Heemstra's decision didn't become apparent until the following spring. In September 1939, Arnhem was a delightful city of historic associations and fine medieval architecture, bordered by lovely woodlands and gentle hills rather than the characteristically dull, flat landscape of the country. In addition to museums, art galleries, historic homes and old churches, there were parks, ablaze with tulips in the spring and summer, and a local symphony orchestra. And, of course, the bridge, to become famous as the scene of a brutal defeat for an Allied invasion.

Arnhem was a city of English

affiliations. Several English families had settled there in the seventeenth century, and the famous poet and soldier Sir Philip Sidney died there. Baroness Van Heemstra became president of the local branch of the British-Netherlands Society, a position that provided fertile ground for sowing the seeds of wartime resistance in which she would soon be heavily engaged.

When Audrey arrived to join her mother and brothers, she found herself living in one of the comfortable family estates just outside the city. She was enrolled at the Arnhem Day School to continue her education, a routine step for a ten-year-old girl, but one that presented her with severe difficulties since she had not learned to speak Dutch. Recalling her first days at the school, she described how she 'sat at my little bench completely baffled. For several days I went home weeping. But I knew I couldn't just give up. I was forced to learn the language quickly. And I did.'

Rather more happily for the girl, her mother arranged for her to pursue her ballet lessons at the Arnhem Conservatory of Music and Dance. If the teaching was undistinguished, it was sufficient to give Audrey a much-needed training in posture, to strengthen her spine, and to loosen up the stiffness which was a heavy liability for a would-be ballerina. Her feet and ankles were weak but, drawing on her characteristic steely determination, she worked at strengthening them sufficiently to allow her to dance on point.

By the spring of 1940, the war clouds were rumbling over Holland. Uniformed soldiers tramped the streets, barbed-wire barricades were erected across the Dutch fields (visible near the Van Heemstra home), the quiet was periodically shattered by gunfire from the borders. That same spring, in the face of serious danger, the Sadler's Wells Ballet was touring Holland and arrived to perform in Arnhem. The courageous company, in the charge of the illustrious choreographer and teacher Ninette (later Dame Ninette) De Valois and conductor Constant Lambert, was headed by Margot Fonteyn, Robert Helpmann and Frederick Ashton. They gave a repertoire that included *The Rake's Progress*, Walton's *Façade*, and *Les Patineurs*.

Their performance was undoubtedly the high point of the starstruck young Audrey's life to date, the occasion further enhanced by the fact that Ella, in her capacity as president of the British-Netherlands Society, hosted the evening. There is a story that exemplifies the atmosphere in which this memorable performance took place.

After the curtain, against a background of increasing gunfire heard in the distance and apparently oblivious of the dangers that were becoming evident to everybody else, the Baroness made a fulsome speech. In addition to the thanks given and the compliments paid, she kept the nervous dancers sitting through a seemingly endless account of the history of Sadler's Wells. That was not all. When she finally wound up her address, Ella announced a late-night supper, at which Audrey was introduced to her idols and presented them with bouquets.

As soon as they decently could, the ballet company fled into their buses, making for the coast and the perilous journey home, but minus scenery, props and costumes which they were forced to leave behind in their efforts to escape the imminent German invasion. There was, however, an explanation for Ella Van Heemstra's behaviour. Aware that there were Nazi supporters in the audience that night, and having already decided to adopt a determinedly unprovocative stance in relation to the Germans, she wished to give the impression that the safety of the English visitors was of little concern to her. It was the first game in the charade that she would play throughout the war, a period when she subtly implied that the Van Heemstra links with the last Kaiser indicated a pro-German bias. With Jewish blood in her veins, Ella could ill afford to antagonise the enemy.

On 10 May 1940, after a night of alarms and sirens, gunfire and falling parachutes, the Germans crossed the Rhine into Holland; on 15 May the Dutch were forced to capitulate. Arnhem, and the rest of the country, was now occupied by the armies of the Third Reich.

FRAILTY AND FORTITUDE

Audrey and fellow hopeful Babs Johnson prepare for their audition for *High Button Shoes*.

2

What I fear most in all the world is war, especially human suffering. During the Nazi occupation . . . I saw so many things which made a lasting impression. But out of it all has come the fact that I am basically optimistic

AUDREY HEPBURN

Audrey Hepburn is the gamine, the urchin, the lost Barnardo boy . . . she is a wistful child of a war-chided era

CECIL BEATON

Audrey Hepburn's steel will was forged in the fires of war. Through five long years, hardship and tragedy held sway in Arnhem, where, in common with the majority of their compatriots throughout the country, people demonstrated high courage, doing whatever was possible to defy Nazi edicts and hide and protect members of their Jewish population. Queen Wilhelmina and her cabinet fled to exile in England. Throughout the war, she broadcast to her suffering subjects on Freedom Radio and became the symbol of their resistance.

Dutch children were forced to confront the horrors of the war; hundreds were active participants, and many died, in the struggle for liberty. Among those who perished was the young Dutch Jewess Anne Frank. Her bravery and lost youth came to serve as an emblem for the fortitude of many of her contemporaries. The eleven-year-old Edda Van Heemstra was one of them and in later years, as Audrey Hepburn the actress, she was repeatedly approached to play her tragic contemporary in the dramatisation of *The Diary of Anne Frank*. It was an obvious choice, but she steadfastly refused. Then, in 1991, in her role as ambassador and fund-raiser for UNICEF, she appeared with the London Symphony Orchestra at London's Barbican concert hall, where she read from Anne Frank's diaries to an orchestral setting composed by the conductor, Michael Tilson Thomas.

The writer and critic Sheridan

Audrey's courageous and tragic contemporary Anne Frank. Note the youthful diarist's poignant and ironic inscription.

Dit is een foto, zoals ik me zou wensen, altijd zo te zijn. Dan had ik nog wel een kans om naar Holywood te komen.

Annefrank.
10 Oct. 1942

(translation)
"This is a photo as I would wish myself to look all the time. Then I would maybe have a chance to come to Hollywood."
Anne Frank, 10 Oct. 1942

Audrey at fourteen,
appearing in a wartime
show to raise funds
for the Resistance.

Morley recalled the occasion: 'Heart-breakingly fragile, looking as though she were made of glass, she stood in front of that huge orchestra and gave a performance of such mesmerising dramatic intensity that afterwards I was not alone in begging her to return to the stage she had left at the time of *Roman Holiday* almost forty years ago.'

She answered Morley, simply and sadly, 'It is not that I am a very good actress, you know; it is just that my family, too, lived under the German occupation of Holland and I knew so many girls like Anne – she would have been about my age. That was why I always declined to make the movie: I knew I would have cried too much.'

At the time, however, there was no room for tears. Initially, Audrey's daily routine continued as before, with the long ride into town to school. Very soon, German language and history were introduced into the curriculum, books censored and teaching appointments made by the Nazis. Their control of the schools spread to all municipal institutions, with Jews, Catholics and those suspected of disloyalty to their regime weeded out and replaced by quislings, of whom Holland – like other occupied countries – had its fair share.

Baroness Van Heemstra dedicated her energies to working for the Resistance, and her daughter was enlisted to help in the carrying of messages, hidden in the soles of her shoes. The ploy was simple and widely used, but one that the Germans discovered. It was a miracle that Audrey escaped detection. Her excellent English, otherwise so carefully concealed, was used on numerous hazardous missions carrying messages to British paratroopers hiding out in the forests at the edge of the city. On one such mission, in the spring of 1942, Audrey was aware of a German patrol in the area. She managed to give her message before making off through the woods and picking wild flowers. As she feared, she encountered a German soldier and, smiling, gave him the flowers. For all the millions her smile was to earn her, this was perhaps its most profitable use.

The Van Heemstras moved into a house at the edge of town, more convenient, much smaller, but inadequately equipped. As the war ground on, Audrey's schooling became sporadic, until she left the Arnhem Day School altogether and continued her lessons with a tutor. Her journeys to and from his house on the other side of town provided cover for her regular errands for the Resistance.

Each day brought fresh difficulties. Audrey's uncle and a cousin were arrested as enemies of the Reich and subsequently executed; then her elder brother, having refused to join the Netherlands Institute for Folkish Education (a euphemistic designation for the Nazi Youth organisation), was sent to a labour camp in Germany for the remainder of the war. These were devastating blows for the Van Heemstras, whose struggle to survive was further increased when, in 1942, the Baroness was stripped of her assets. The family properties were confiscated and her bank accounts sequestered, leaving her to support her family on a meagre allowance 'given' to her by the German authorities.

For Audrey there were none of the pleasures or pangs of a normal adolescence, no parties, no picnics, no teenage romances. There was no cinema (she confessed in later years never to have heard of Hollywood) other than the propaganda films, often virulently anti-Semitic, that were churned out in Germany. In 1943, the Germans confiscated all civilian radios, leaving the Dutch isolated from the outside world. They listened to their Queen's broadcasts on illegal transmitters – secretly, and on pain of death.

At least there was music, albeit only that of Austro-German composers. Mozart, Beethoven and Wagner, however, transcended the bleak spirit of the time, and Audrey turned more and more to

music as her only means of escape from the realities of her daily life.

She continued to attend the Arnhem Conservatory, which, by 1943, had become an important front for a particular area of underground activity. Behind the public façade of music and dance, Resistance workers organised food, shelter and forged documents for Dutch patriots in danger. Concerts, dance recitals and other entertainments were held, and the money siphoned off to fund the Resistance. In addition to her lessons and arduous barre practice, Audrey participated in the ballet recitals.

This method of raising money was expanded by the staging of recitals in private homes. Since the audience at these venues generally comprised a larger number of people than was permitted by the Nazis to gather in one place, they were nerve-racking occasions, held behind locked doors and closed curtains, with the accompanying piano played at the lowest level of audibility in order to escape detection.

Clothes, material and ballet shoes were desperately scarce, and costumes had to be improvised. Hungry and gaunt, Audrey was none the less shooting up in height, which robbed her of some of the more romantic roles she would have liked to dance. As she recalled, 'I never was a raindrop, though I was dying to be. I was a "boy". I had to lift up the little girls because I was so tall.'

Tall she certainly was, but also – with increasing privation – stick-thin and anaemic, and suffering from asthma attacks and the occasional fainting spell. Scarcity of food had become a severe problem in Holland and even the already inadequate diet of watery soup with a little bread was in short supply. At one stage Audrey lived for a whole month on endives – she never ate an endive again – and, during the spring, she and her brother Ian found sustenance in tulip bulbs dug from the fields. Many people ate cooked grass, something that she could never bring herself to do.

Finally, in the last phase of the war, Audrey was forced to stop dancing. Even her extraordinary determination was insufficient to overcome the frailty of her malnourished body. She witnessed many appalling events. Accustomed from early in the Occupation to the sight of Jews of all ages forced to wear the yellow Star of David, she now saw them rounded up for their deportation to the death camps.

The memory of these scenes never left her. Some thirty years later, from the haven of her home

Members of the British Allied Airborne Division take up position in the woods on the outskirts of Arnhem – a prelude to the fatal battle.

in Switzerland, she told American journalist Curtis Bill Pepper, 'I saw families with little children, with babies, herded into meat wagons – trains of big wooden vans with just a little slat open at the top and all those faces peering out at you . . . on the platform were soldiers herding more Jewish families with their poor little bundles and small children. There would be families together and they would separate them, saying the men go there and the women go there. Then they would take the babies and put them in another van . . . All the nightmares I've ever had are mingled with that.'

The final nine months of the war were the most gruelling of all for the now fifteen-year-old Audrey. On 17 September 1944, immediately after the German collapse in Normandy, the First British Airborne Division was parachuted into Holland to undertake Operation Market Garden. This was the Allied plan, under General Montgomery, to cut off the bridges of Holland and secure the crossing of the Rhine into Germany.

After the war.

The bridge at Arnhem was one of the most strategically significant targets, but things went horribly wrong when the British forces earmarked to take it ran into two armoured SS panzer divisions. One British battalion managed to fight through to the bridge but, once there, they were cut off and forced into bloody retreat. This was 'the bridge too far', as one general called it – thence the title for Richard Attenborough's epic movie version of the events.

The disaster of the bridge brought the fighting into the city, whose inhabitants became the victims of the Battle of Arnhem. Great swathes of Arnhem were laid waste, while its beleaguered citizens crammed themselves into cellars along with wounded and dying British soldiers, whom they tended as best they could. On 23 September, the head of the local Red Cross was summoned by a German officer and ordered to evacuate the city. All those living south of the railway were to be gone by eight o'clock that night, the rest by the following day.

Protest proved useless and, within thirty-six hours, 100,000 people, bearing babies and bundles and wheeling bicycles in the sad tradition of refugees, streamed out of the city. Ella Van Heemstra,

Baroness Ella Van Heemstra and her daughter in 1946.

her daughter Audrey and her younger son, Ian, were among them. Three thousand died *en route*. To this day, military historians have been unable to discover who gave this order, or why. Apparently the overall Commander of the German forces in Arnhem knew nothing about it.

The Van Heemstras were fortunate in finding accommodation very quickly in a large, rambling house in the country. They were not alone, however: more than two hundred refugees shared the same premises, struggling together for survival. Audrey lived in these worsening conditions for some months until word of the Allied advance began to filter through.

In a gesture of brave and defiant solidarity, thousands of Arnhem's refugees trekked back to the city to welcome their liberators, who did not arrive for several weeks. The Germans were now running scared and did not bar the people from the city. Rather, they embarked on a programme of picking people off the streets at random to service the manpower shortage in their institutions. One of those was Audrey, pulled into a group of girls destined to work in the kitchens.

However, in a scenario worthy of the kind of films she later resisted making, while the girls stood in the street waiting to be marched off, the officer in charge turned his back for a moment. In a flash of quick thinking and reckless bravery, Audrey fled, and hid herself in the nearest abandoned cellar. Cold and hungry, she passed her days in darkness and isolation, growing ill and weak. Incredibly, she stayed in hiding for more than three weeks, emerging shaken and suffering from hepatitis.

On 5 May 1945, the day after her birthday, Holland was liberated. The sixteen-year-old girl was now five foot seven inches tall. She suffered from malnutrition, her ankles were swollen with oedema, and she weighed just ninety pounds. Her frail condition did not prevent her from joining in the joyous welcome of the Allied troops. Their presence meant not only the end of gunfire and the exodus of the hated Nazis, but the arrival of food parcels (including chocolates). Describing her feelings on the day the Allies arrived, Hepburn maintained, 'That was the day I learned that freedom has a bouquet, a perfume all its own — that smell of English tobacco.'

The happiest event for the Van Heemstras was the return of Alexander from Germany, but with Ella's houses virtually demolished in the fighting, and little money available, Arnhem held few prospects. Ella decided that they should go to Amsterdam. An accomplished cook, she found herself a job as cook-housekeeper to a well-off Amsterdam family, and organised a small flat for herself and her children.

Life in Amsterdam was lived with few frills. The Baroness's wages were just enough to pay the rent and see that her family did not go hungry. Audrey remained frail, weakened by her wartime existence, but her dancing ambitions were undimmed and her determination was stronger than ever. Somehow her remarkable mother managed to scrape together enough money to pay for classes with Sonia Gaskell, a highly gifted White Russian teacher renowned for her imagination and her discipline.

Audrey's upper arms were so thin that Madame Gaskell could close her own small hands round them. She worried about her new pupil's physical fragility, but quickly recognised her iron will to succeed. Audrey worked with intense dedication, blossoming under Sonia Gaskell's sympathetic tutelage. She perfected her posture, developed her poise and her concentration; her flat body and delicate face with its high cheekbones and huge eyes gave her the look of a ballerina. Her one natural disadvantage, which she was powerless to alter, was her height.

Her passion for music continued, and she longed to attend concerts at Amsterdam's Concertgebouw. Mengelberg, the wartime conductor of the Concertgebouw orchestra, had employed Nazi collaborators and had performed for the Germans throughout the Occupation. Having been branded a traitor, he had gone into exile in Switzerland, and the orchestra was enjoying an immediate post-war renaissance under Eduard Van Beinum. On Audrey's seventeenth birthday, her mother gave her a six-month season ticket for the concerts; at Christmas, the present was a ticket for a series of Beethoven quartets. One can only marvel at the Baroness's efforts in saving sufficient money to pay for the treasured tickets. Certainly, there was no money for tram fares, and Audrey had to walk the considerable distance to and from the concert hall.

Late in 1947, an unexpected event brought excitement and a little extra money to Audrey. The Dutch producer-director team of H.M. Josephson and Huguenot Van der Linden were making a short film called *Nederland in 7 Lessen* (*Dutch in 7 Lessons*) and were looking for a girl to play the small part of an air hostess. The film has long been consigned to obscurity and the facts of Audrey's involvement differ substantially in various accounts. One story goes that producer and director visited Madame Gaskell's academy to look for a poised young woman; another maintains that a mutual acquaintance of the Van Heemstras and Van Der Linden sent her to see the director in his apartment. Whatever the truth of it, the result was the same: Audrey Hepburn went in front of a film camera for the first time in the tiny role of a KLM stewardess.

Audrey was delighted at having been chosen. She enjoyed the experience and was a few guilders better off, but it did not occur to her that film acting might be a possible career. It was her ambition to continue her studies in London with the celebrated Marie (later Dame Marie) Rambert. When Sonia Gaskell announced that she would be closing her studio and moving to Paris, Audrey found the spur to her intent. Her mother agreed that the time had come for her daughter to take serious steps towards achieving her goals. There were sufficient funds only for the boat tickets and to keep them from immediate destitution but, undaunted, in 1948, they departed for England – the country Audrey had left nine years earlier.

The Baroness Van Heemstra and her nineteen-year-old daughter arrived in London by the boat-train. Having settled in a cheap little hotel near King's Cross, they set off to find the Mercury Theatre, a converted church hall in Notting Hill Gate that was home to the Ballet Rambert and its adjoining school.

Famed for her unorthodox approach both to dance and to its would-be practitioners, Marie Rambert was revered for her inspirational gifts. Although sixty years old in 1948, she showed no signs of flagging, either personally or professionally. She had been born in Warsaw and studied dance first with Isadora Duncan's brother in Paris in the early 1900s, then with Émile Dalcroze in Geneva. The young Marie Rambert's training with Dalcroze (who taught his own systems of movement in relation to musical

Dame Marie Rambert, the formidable founder of the ballet company that bears her name, fondly known to her students as Mim.

structures) fitted her for membership of Diaghilev's famous Ballets Russes, which she joined in 1912. She danced with the company and trained with its ballet master, the brilliant Cecchetti, but her main assignment was to work with Nijinsky on the complex rhythms of Stravinsky's *The Rite of Spring*, of which the Diaghilev company gave the legendary world première in 1913.

When war broke out in 1914, Rambert went to England. She married the English playwright and critic Ashley Dukes, and opened a dancing school which was to develop into the Ballet Rambert. Her contribution to British ballet was incalculable. She particularly encouraged the development of budding choreographers; among her young dance students, Antony Tudor,

Andrée Howard, Walter Gore and Frederick Ashton were her successful protégés.

Dark and bird-like, voluble and eccentric, she was a sympathetic and sensitive woman, but also a famously harsh disciplinarian: any sloppiness of deportment on the part of a pupil was rewarded with a painful rap on the knuckles. This was delivered with the stick she always carried and which she also used for emphasis, banging it on the wooden floors of the school studio – a bare space, containing the barre and a battered upright piano, where the prevailing gloom was slightly relieved by stained-glass windows.

After an interview with Ella and Audrey, Madame Rambert put Audrey through the paces of a rigorous audition and was sufficiently impressed with her prowess to accept her into the school. However, the matter of fees proved difficult until Rambert, assessing the situation, offered a scholarship.

This was Audrey's first stroke of good fortune, but one that did not solve the problem of living expenses since the scholarship covered only tuition. In an additional gesture of generosity, Marie Rambert offered to take Audrey into her own home, a large house in Campden Hill Square which she shared with her husband and their Irish housekeeper, who mothered Madame's young hopefuls.

In 1983, a gala tribute to Dame Marie Rambert, who had died at the age of ninety-four, was held at the Sadler's Wells Theatre. Audrey flew to London to take part in the evening. She spoke of herself as 'a failed ballerina', and told the capacity audience, composed of the ballet-world élite, 'I owe her [Rambert] a great deal. She was a great inspiration and a wonderful friend to me.'

While Audrey attended classes from ten in the morning until six in the evening, Ella eked out a living in a succession of modest jobs that began with work in a florist's shop. After several months, she became the manager of a small block of flats in Mayfair, where she was able to rent a room at a concessionary rate. In due course, she secured an apartment in the same building which enabled Audrey to leave the Rambert household and live with her. For the next few years, 65 South Audley Street was their home.

Audrey worked at her ballet with the absolute dedication that not only characterised her, but was demanded by Madame Rambert of her pupils. One of the incidental pleasures that came with attending the Rambert school was being allowed in to see the professional company's dress rehearsals at the charming little Mercury Theatre. But life was hard in 1948. London was still in the grip of post-war rationing, food was scarce and the city bore the terrible scars of the Blitz. While Audrey's major preoccupation was to succeed as a dancer, she was also profoundly concerned to earn enough money to keep herself. She was neither acquisitive nor extravagant – even in later life, when she became a millionaire, she lived simply and unostentatiously. But the war had left her desperately insecure and the quest for material security was to prove a decisive factor in several of her most important decisions.

In addition to full-time classes, Audrey took whatever odd jobs she could find after hours. These included a particularly depressing stint in a nightclub, holding up placards to announce the acts. Rather more lucrative and rewarding, albeit tiring, were the assignments she began to pick up as a model for magazine photographers – work that fed her interest in fashion and her feeling for style. While the money made some difference to her meagre existence, it was not sufficient and, although progressing well in her classes, she began to question whether she was good *enough*. For

Audrey, to succeed meant to reach
the top – to be another Fonteyn,
not merely a member of the *corps
de ballet*. As the months went by,
she became increasingly conscious
that her height might prove an
obstacle to her ambitions.

Marie Rambert's opinion of her
pupil was high: 'She was such a
good worker, a wonderful learner.
If she had wanted to persevere in
ballet, she might have become an
outstanding ballerina.' But,
echoing Audrey's own misgivings,
she added, 'It was because of her
height that I couldn't consider her
for my company.'

Looking back to this time,
Audrey reflected, 'I had found
that my height was a handicap in
ballet and I might have to slave
for years to achieve only limited
success. I couldn't wait years; I
needed money badly.'

That need led her to attend a
casting call for the London
production of *High Button Shoes*, a
hit Broadway musical composed
by Jule Styne. The demands of
musical comedy were unfamiliar to
the ballet student, but her special
aura drew people to her, working
its particular spell at the auditions.
To her amazement, she was one of
ten girls chosen for the chorus.

This venture into uncharted
territory effectively marked the
end of Hepburn's dream of
becoming a prima ballerina.

With Babs Johnson
again, waiting in the
wings before the *High
Button Shoes* audition.

STEPPING OUT

On point in *Secret People*, the last expression of her classical-ballet aspirations.

3

From the age of six to twenty, I dreamed of only one thing: to be a dancer

AUDREY HEPBURN

God's gift to publicity men is a heart-shattering young woman with a style of her own . . . The name is Audrey Hepburn; and some people have been twenty-four times to Ciro's to see her cabaret performance . . .

PICTUREGOER

On 22 December 1948, *High Button Shoes* opened at the London Hippodrome, where it ran for 291 performances. With a score by Jule Styne and choreography by Jerome Robbins, it was no easy show for the chorus. The story concerned the escapades of a 1920s con man, and the big numbers drew their inspiration from dances of the period, such as the Charleston, and from the screen antics of the Keystone Kops and Mack Sennett's Bathing Beauties.

It was, in every particular, a new world and a new challenge for Audrey. With her classical ballet training and limited performing experience, she was not ideally equipped for the pyrotechnics of a fast and furious American musical comedy; she had to work hard to overcome her stiffness and fit in with the ensemble of practised show dancers. Dressing-room relationships, too, were conducted in a language of gossip, giggles and exchanges of confidence foreign to Audrey. Her background was very different from those of her fellow chorines, and she was inexperienced in the ways of their world. At nineteen, she was yet to have a boyfriend or fall in love.

She was, in short, an outsider. None the less, as she learned the ropes, she began to enjoy the atmosphere of the theatre, and she certainly enjoyed receiving a weekly pay packet containing eight pounds and ten shillings.

Whenever possible, she attended classes at the Rambert school, and she also put herself through a weekly keep-fit routine at a London gym. She was sometimes accompanied by a friend from the chorus of the show, a long-legged beauty named Kay Kendall, who was also later to become a star, marrying Rex Harrison before her tragic death of leukaemia at the age of thirty-three.

By the time of her twentieth birthday in May 1949, Audrey had bade farewell to the ballet school – it was simply not realistic to continue. The London run of *High Button Shoes* closed in the spring of 1949. Audrey declined to join the national tour, but she was not unemployed for long. Producer Cecil Landau had noticed her in the chorus at the Hippodrome and been dazzled by her smile and the strength of personality that came across the footlights – although he told English journalist Logan Gourlay, 'The first impression was made by a pair of big dark eyes and a fringe flitting across the stage.'

A difficult and temperamental man, Landau was also a gifted impresario and a canny talent-spotter. He staged revues of a lavishness unseen since C.B. Cochran's extravaganzas in the 1920s and early 1930s, taking expensive risks, and was no stranger to debt and the law courts.

When *High Button Shoes* closed, Landau was about to go into rehearsal with an ambitious new revue called *Sauce Tartare*. He had spent almost a year gathering together an international cast from as far afield as Russia and South Africa. There were featured artists from Norway and Spain, from Holland and Belgium, and a calypso band from Trinidad. The star of the show was the black American singer Muriel Smith, who had shot to fame on Broadway in *Carmen Jones* six years previously, and who was to sing Bizet's *Carmen* in the 1956-57 season at Covent Garden.

The revue, which cost twenty-five thousand pounds – a massive sum in those days – opened at the Cambridge Theatre on 18 May 1949. Audrey was a member of the small chorus on a salary of ten pounds a week. She continued to inflict a punishing schedule on herself: in addition to performing in the show, she pursued her photographic modelling assignments, joined a Saturday-morning movement class for actors, and kept up her barre practice. She also began taking private classes with Felix (later Sir Felix) Aylmer. A fine character actor, who had played Polonius to Laurence Olivier's screen Hamlet, he schooled Audrey in diction and 'taught me to concentrate intelligently on what I was doing, and made me aware that all actors need a method of sorts to be even vaguely professional'.

Audrey later recalled this period of her life as one of confusion. 'When I think of myself at twenty, I was very much at sea. I wasn't at all sure what life was all about,' she said.

Society photographer Anthony Beauchamp saw *Sauce Tartare*. He had photographed some notable beauties on both sides of the Atlantic, among them Vivien Leigh and Garbo; his striking study of his future wife, Sarah Churchill, featured on the cover of *Life* magazine, had made an impression. Beauchamp, too, was struck by 'the chorus girl with the eyes'. He sought Audrey out backstage, and became instrumental in making her face a familiar fixture of the smart fashion magazines.

Despite its rave reviews, *Sauce Tartare* ran out of steam early in 1950. Almost immediately, the irrepressible Landau began rehearsals for a follow-up revue, and re-engaged Audrey. Aware that she had attracted more

attention than was customary for a chorus girl, he gave her featured spots in several sketches and set pieces, raising her salary to fifteen pounds a week. *Sauce Piquante* opened at the Cambridge on 27 April 1950. Muriel Smith was once again the singing star; others in the large cast included Moira Lister, Joan Heal, Norman Wisdom, Bob Monkhouse and a handsome, moody French crooner named Marcel Le Bon.

Bob Monkhouse, who befriended Audrey, recalled, 'The standard of dancing in *Sauce Piquante* was of a superior quality, but Audrey's was the poorest dancing in the show. If she'd been a good dancer, the other girls would not have minded so much, but everyone knew that she was the least talented among them. They all loved her offstage, but hated her on, because they knew that even if she just jumped up and down, the audience would still be attracted to her. What Audrey had in *Sauce Piquante*, and what has sustained her through a fantastically successful career, was an enormous exaggerated feeling of "I need you".'

Monkhouse also recalled the applause she received at every performance when the curtain rose to reveal her as a Dresden shepherdess. All she did was stand on the stage in her beautiful

costume, but 'it was quite extraordinary. She simply signalled that infectious, impish grin, which seemed to go from one earhole to the other. She looked incredibly radiant . . .'

Testimony to her smile, her eyes, her 'glow', has been given by dozens of people, audience and fellow performers alike, who remember her from those days. At the same time she was making an impression on publicists, and her face, though not her name, was soon known throughout Britain as that of the Lacto-Calamine girl, looking down from hoardings and out from the pages of magazines.

Although *Sauce Piquante* had been well received, audience attendance was poor. The lack of business was blamed on the heat wave that had descended on the country, but whatever the cause, Landau was forced to close the show after a mere sixty-seven performances, leaving himself with a massive financial loss. During the short run, however, Audrey had her first recorded taste of romance. Marcel Le Bon began sending roses to the stage door on her twenty-first birthday. Soon, they were spending a great deal of time together – to the chagrin of Landau, who feared losing his treasured Audrey. He announced the addition of a 'no marriage' clause to the contracts of his four junior principals, of whom Audrey was one. She, apparently, found this amusing.

Undaunted by the closure of *Piquante* and determined to rescue what he could, Landau rejigged the revue in a potted version with a slimmed-down cast and arranged to present it at Ciro's, one of London's most fashionable nightclubs. Audrey was to remain as part of a four-girl line-up; Marcel Le Bon was told that his services were no longer required.

Retitled *Summer Nights*, the dazzling late-night revue opened at Ciro's in July 1950. Encountered in the comparatively intimate confines of cabaret, Audrey Hepburn began causing something of a sensation among people in the entertainment business who visited Ciro's that summer. Each night brought somebody who was bowled over by her presence and felt that he or she (usually he) was the first to discover this strangely bewitching creature.

Stanley Holloway, who would one day play Alfred Doolittle to Audrey's Eliza in the film of *My Fair Lady*, comments in his autobiography on the remarkable number of people at that time who 'genuinely kidded themselves into believing that they were the first to recognise Audrey's potential radiant talent'.

The object of this excitement, meanwhile, was living happily with her mother in South Audley Street, getting home from Ciro's well after two in the morning, and sleeping until noon. Landau's precautions notwithstanding, she was still seeing Marcel Le Bon. He, and a handful of others out of a job after *Sauce Piquante*, were putting together a cabaret of their own which they planned to take on tour. Audrey had agreed to join them and spent many afternoons working with the group.

Among those who responded to her at Ciro's were a few who expressed their enthusiasm in a practical way. The Australian actor John McCallum and his actress wife Googie Withers, stars of several British films, were so impressed with Audrey that McCallum phoned his agent, who subsequently signed her up. It was a breakthrough for her since, incredibly, other agents had turned her down. McCallum recalled the occasion when he first saw Audrey: 'We had a table near the cabaret and I found that I couldn't take my eyes off one of the dancing girls. Nothing unusual in that, but this girl – Audrey Hepburn – was different. She had large, doe-like eyes, and an elfin look. But what set her apart from the others was a certain indescribable kind of *élan*, which generated magnetism.'

The McCallums' friends Michael Denison and Dulcie Gray shared this opinion, and passed the word to Robert Lennard, the casting director at Associated British Pictures. Lennard's nose for star quality was the sharpest in the business. He was internationally known and respected, and had influenced the course of many British acting careers. Hepburn's quality was at once apparent to him. He arranged an appointment at his office in Soho, but his colleagues at Associated British were unimpressed with the youthful, flat-chested girl.

He had better luck with director Mario Zampi, on the look-out for a fresh face for his next production. Despatched to Ciro's by Lennard, Zampi showed an enthusiasm for Audrey which encouraged him to see the show several times – legend estimates the number of his visits at anything between fourteen and twenty-four – and arranged an interview with her. Despite her total lack of acting experience, Zampi and screenwriter Michael Pertwee were confident that she could carry off a leading role and made an offer accordingly.

Laughter in Paradise, released in 1951, is British screen comedy at its best. The plot turns on the will

With Guy Middleton in *Laughter in Paradise*. Her bit part led to a contract with Associated British.

Posing for a publicity shot on the English coast, 1951.

of an eccentric practical joker who leaves his fortune to be divided among his relatives. There is a proviso, however: each has to carry out a series of instructions that are variously embarrassing, impossible, impractical or criminal.

The film is beautifully written, deftly directed, and played for all its worth by an all-star cast headed by Alastair Sim, Fay Compton and Joyce Grenfell. In the plot, amoral playboy Simon Russell (Guy Middleton) is ordered to marry the first girl he speaks to after the reading of the will. Strictly speaking, his bride should be the cigarette girl in a nightclub he frequents, but he ignores the fact that he exchanges a couple of words with her, and courts Lucille Grayson, a supposed upper-class heiress. She turns out to be his butler's niece, who is conning him as much as he is conning her. This was the part originally offered to Hepburn.

To Zampi's astonishment and her mother's intense disappointment, Audrey turned down this offer in favour of going on the road with Marcel and his revue. (It is not known whether Cecil Landau was aware of this plan. Audrey was still playing nights at Ciro's.) However, the bookings failed to materialise, sending the moody Marcel into a black depression and Audrey back

A fleeting appearance with Alec Guinness (left) in *The Lavender Hill Mob*.

to Zampi's office at Associated British. By then, the role of Lucille had gone to Beatrice Campbell, but Audrey happily accepted a day's work as the cigarette girl. By the time filming started, her infatuation with Marcel was a thing of the past and he had left for the USA.

Audrey's two tiny scenes in *Laughter in Paradise* gave her only a few words to speak, but Pinewood Studios was buzzing with talk of her. Eleanor Summerfield recalled that 'everyone who had seen the rushes . . . were [sic] quite convinced that a new star had arrived.' Looking at the film now, one realises that Audrey's guardian angel must

have been protecting her: while she would undoubtedly have been delicious as Lucille Grayson, deliciousness is not what was called for, and she was too young and unsophisticated to have been as convincing as the older, more experienced Miss Campbell.

Instead, with the billing 'Introducing Audrey Hepburn', she made an entrancing cigarette girl, and she was offered a seven-year contract by Associated British on the strength of it. Curiously, the company did very little with her, giving the impression that the studio executives had forgotten why they had wanted her on the payroll. After a blink-and-you'll-miss-it bit

in *One Wild Oat*, the film version of a West End farce, she was loaned to Ealing Studios for *The Lavender Hill Mob*. In this enduring classic from the Ealing comedy collection she was Chiquita, a chic, but entirely unexplained, young woman to whom Alec Guinness hands some money in a Rio restaurant some two minutes into the film. She says, 'Oh – but I – how sweet of you,' gives him a thank-you kiss on the temple, and exits, never to be seen again. If audiences, not surprisingly, still didn't know who she was, Guinness was very impressed with her – so much so that he persuaded American producer-director Mervyn LeRoy

Top: With Joan Greenwood and Nigel Patrick in *Young Wives' Tale*.

Above: With Valentina Cortesa in *Secret People*.

Audrey's role, her first featured part, the silliest ingredient of all. She played a young woman who fantasises that she is being followed by every man who looks at her, but, despite the feeble script and her evident inexperience, the voltage rises when she makes her entrance. Years later, Joan Greenwood told writer Boze Hadleigh, 'I thought Miss Hepburn was enchanting, and that it was only a matter of time until she too would find her niche. She had . . . a splendid voice.' As Hadleigh notes, the mellifluousness of the Hepburn voice was compared, early in her career, to Miss Greenwood's own famously distinctive, husky and somewhat mannered vocal quality.

All four of these films were released in England, but not the USA, in 1951, the year Audrey made *Secret People*, again on loan to Ealing, for the distinguished British director Thorold Dickinson. The film is a somewhat confused but none the less interesting espionage thriller with a clear anti-Fascist message, set in the 1930s. Nora (Angela Fouldes), a little Italian girl, and her older sister Maria (Valentina Cortesa), are sent to live in England, leaving their father behind to continue the fight for freedom in Italy. A few years later, Maria's fiancé, Louis (Serge Reggiani),

to see her for the female lead for *Quo Vadis?* She was given a screen test by MGM, but the part went to Deborah Kerr.

Yet another comedy followed. Directed by Henry Cass, *Young Wives' Tale* wasted the talents of a cast that included Joan Greenwood, Nigel Patrick, Derek Farr, Athene Seyler and Irene Handl. It is a silly and undistinguished film, with whom she had thought she would never see again, reappears in their lives and turns out to be the leader of a group of ruthless saboteurs. Nora — now grown into a teenager, played by twenty-two-year-old Audrey Hepburn — is an aspiring ballerina, and both she and Maria are used by Louis as dupes in a plot to blow up a visiting German dignitary. It all ends in tragedy, but not before Audrey gets to dance on point three times in the course of the film. In the last dancing scene she is partnered by John Field.

Choreographer and teacher Andrée Howard, one of Madame Rambert's associates who had worked with Audrey at the ballet school, was instrumental in getting her the part of Nora, but not before endless delays and casting indecisions. Dickinson wanted Audrey but considered her too tall, especially next to Italian actress Lea Padovani, who was to play her big sister. It was only when negotiations fell through and Padovani was replaced by Cortese that Howard's influence prevailed. Rehearsals were arduous and made more so by being held in cold and draughty premises, while filming involved outdoor shooting at night, which took place in a freezing April drizzle. All of Audrey's physical and mental stamina was required to withstand these conditions and rise to the occasion of dancing with somebody of Field's calibre. Nora was her biggest and most difficult part to date and she played it with a fresh and charming sincerity. Her dancing, too, was excellent, but the performance is marred by some gauche and squeaky delivery of lines.

It was not only work that was going well for Audrey. She had a new, and seriously intentioned, admirer. James Hanson, a tall, elegant, twenty-nine-year-old Yorkshireman, was the son of a wealthy Huddersfield businessman who had made his money in trucking. Hanson's own businesses in England and Canada would later develop into an international industrial empire, making him a multimillionaire and bringing him a title (Lord Hanson). In 1951 he was the archetypal upper middle-class Englishman: an ex-officer of the Duke of Wellington's regiment who had served in the war, he was a keen huntsman, horseman, yachtsman and golfer. He was cultivated, too, enjoying the theatre and the cinema, and was a trustee of the D'Oyly Carte Opera.

Hanson loved fast cars and beautiful women — he had recently been Jean Simmons's escort — and frequented the most fashionable nightspots in London. He had a reputation as something of a playboy, but fell very much in love with Audrey. She was beguiled by his debonair charm and air of masculine strength — the qualities that would attract her to all the men in her life — and the couple were soon the object of gossip-column interest.

Baroness Van Heemstra, although she always kept a low profile in relation to Audrey's work, was determined that her daughter should be a success and was much against her involvement with her new beau. She did not consider that life as a social hostess in the wilds of Yorkshire, entertaining the hunting, shooting, fishing set, was a suitable destiny for her daughter, and made her disapproval known. It was a difficult situation for Audrey. She was caught not only between the opposing forces of her mother and Jimmy, but in the conflict of her own needs and desires. On the one hand, she was driven by her professional ambitions; on the other, she longed for love and stability, while sharing her mother's doubts as to the suitability of life as Hanson's wife.

Meanwhile, Associated British had been asked for a girl to appear in a film to be shot simultaneously in French and English, on location in Monte Carlo. With her fluent French, Audrey was ideal and, although the part was once again very small and the film yet another forgettable comedy, the temptation of seeing the Riviera and spending time in the sun proved irresistible. Even James Hanson, who was now talking of marriage, could not stop Audrey from accepting the job. Accompanied by Baroness Van Heemstra, she arrived in France for the first time, and set to work on *Nous Irons à Monte Carlo*, or *Monte Carlo Baby* – in either language it has been long forgotten – filming her main scene in the lobby of the Hôtel de Paris.

Staying at this hotel as the guests of Prince Rainier were the renowned French novelist Colette and her husband, Maurice Goudeket. By then in her late seventies, Colette was frail, crippled with arthritis and confined to a wheelchair. She was also much preoccupied with a proposed stage production of her famous last novel, *Gigi*, which Anita (*Gentlemen Prefer Blondes*) Loos had adapted for New York impresario Gilbert Miller. Plans to proceed with the Broadway show had been halted by the difficulty of finding the right actress for the

title role – somebody sufficiently young and fresh to be convincing as an innocent teenager, yet capable of flowering into young womanhood. The part calls for looks lovely enough to attract a sophisticated Parisian womaniser, and the acting ability to make a difficult emotional transition from *soi-disant* courtesan to young woman in love.

One morning, to pass the time, Colette asked to watch the filming in the hotel. She saw Audrey at work and was instantly convinced that she had found her actress. As Audrey recalled in an interview with *Cinémonde* some years later, 'She was watching the filming from her wheelchair in a corner of the hall. When it was finished she came up to me and said in a very loud voice, "You are my Gigi," and everything took off from there.'

Events now overtook Audrey with bewildering rapidity. Aware of her total lack of stage acting experience, she was overwhelmed by doubts and initially inclined to refuse the challenge. Colette remained convinced that hard work would see her through, and cabled Gilbert Miller and Anita Loos. Audrey met the rich, successful and powerful producer in his suite at the Savoy. He recognised the suitability of her looks and personality for the role

AUDREY HEPBURN · JULES MUNSHIN · RAY VENTURA AND HIS ORCHESTRA IN
MONTE CARLO BABY
GFD
'U'

of Gigi, but had misgivings about her technical capabilities. Loos arrived in London a couple of days later with her travelling companion, the actress Paulette Goddard. Miller had left a portfolio of pictures of Audrey in their suite. When the women looked at the photographs, Goddard remarked, 'She's too perfect. There's got to be something wrong – perhaps she lisps.'

When Audrey came to see Loos, Goddard was present. Both women were entranced by this delicate, gazelle-like creature, simply and stunningly dressed in a black skirt and flat shoes, with a man's shirt tied around the waist. Anita had no hesitation in endorsing Colette's choice, but Miller remained worried. He arranged for his friend the splendid veteran actress Cathleen Nesbitt to listen to Audrey read from the stage of a London theatre. She was virtually inaudible. Miss Nesbitt, however, was confident that Audrey could be taught voice projection and offered to coach her at her home just outside New York City, to which she was returning.

This was good enough for Miller. The complex negotiations of sorting out Audrey's contractual arrangements with Associated British Pictures were set in motion. While the lawyers

Audrey and the famous French novelist Colette, who set her on the road to stardom.

haggled, Paramount Pictures asked Audrey to test for a new film to be made by William Wyler, who was searching for a young unknown non-American girl to star in it. The test was successfully made, but while Paramount held fire on their casting decisions, Audrey prepared to leave for America.

She was now excited by the prospect of *Gigi*, and committed to rising to its difficult challenge. James Hanson was rather less pleased by the turn of events. It was a difficult parting, tempered by Audrey's agreeing to marriage when the run of *Gigi* ended.

Opposite: A scene from the obscure *Monte Carlo Baby*, during the making of which she met Colette.

1951

A sceptical Gigi.

Opposite: Becoming acquainted with the delights of the courtesan's jewel-box.

Audrey left for New York at the beginning of October and took up residence at the Blackstone Hotel, in a room next door to David Niven and his wife. She was immediately plunged into an exhausting schedule of rehearsals as well as lessons with Cathleen Nesbitt, who, to Audrey's delight, had been cast as Gigi's great-aunt. Her introduction to the legitimate stage was, however, fraught with difficulties. During the sea voyage from England, she had gorged herself on pastries, puddings and her beloved chocolates. According to Anita Loos's biographer, Gary Carey, 'The sprite Miller had hired in London was now a very tubby gamine.' Miller was horrified and Audrey was ordered on to a strict diet, which in the course of rehearsals she carried too far, leaving herself disastrously enervated. Miller's wife, Kitty, was called in to take the girl under her wing and make sure she was properly nourished.

David Niven, who became a close friend of Audrey's, recalled that 'Audrey was alone and, I think, very lonely . . . she was probably far more relaxed than I was, probably because she knew that she was headed for an immense triumph and I knew that I was headed for an absolute disaster. [He was to open – and

close – in *Nina* with Gloria Swanson.] However, we both had the maximum amount of first-night nerves and panic to compete with. She always seemed divine, of course, to look at – and gave the impression of being vulnerable.'

George Cukor had originally been down to direct the play, but had pulled out, to be replaced by Raymond Rouleau, Belgian-born and Paris-based. A charming, gifted and successful stage and screen director, Rouleau spoke no English. Anita's script was translated back into French and the cast found themselves effectively rehearsing in one language to play in another. The distinguished Constance Collier, playing Gigi's grandmother, couldn't take the strain and left; her replacement, Florence Reed, went the same way. (Josephine Hull finally played the part.) Audrey's superb French was no help to her in perfecting the correct inflections in English. Nervous and tired, she was at first alarmingly inadequate, a state of affairs of which Rouleau was all too aware, and which he took drastic steps to correct.

Years later, Rouleau's widow wrote an account of events to Audrey's 1984 biographer, Charles Higham: 'The first eight days of work with Audrey were truly terrible: Audrey had no idea what

she was doing. She was acting extremely badly, totally failing to understand the meaning of the text . . . Finally, my late husband, who was growing totally disturbed, on the eighth day took Audrey aside for a private meeting, and told her quite firmly that she must improve or else. She must work with more dedication, obtain enough sleep, eat properly, devote herself to the text and, in a word, become properly professional or he would decline all responsibility for her future on Broadway and in the production itself. He was very severe with her . . .'

This is the only recorded instance of Audrey's commitment and, indeed, care of herself, being questioned. Certainly, she was as dedicated as ever, and one must assume that her inexperience, punishing schedule, absence from her mother and Jimmy, and coping with the overwhelming impact of New York for the first time, had taken a toll. But the measure of her will to succeed is clear. Mrs Rouleau's letter continued, 'Next day, a new Audrey emerged. She understood everything that Raymond had told her. From that moment she progressed steadily, and became better and better every day, using every bit of advice Raymond had given her . . . she suddenly emerged as the fine professional

she was to remain for the rest of her career.'

James Hanson, who spent much time at his Canadian office, came to New York as often as he could and, once her play was running, Audrey would sometimes fly to Toronto to spend Sundays with him. On 4 December 1951, their engagement was announced in the London *Times*. Other than spending time with Jimmy, Audrey kept herself largely to herself, continuing her lessons with Cathleen Nesbitt and conserving her energies for her performance. Pursuing a policy that would remain consistent throughout her career, she steadfastly avoided the social-theatrical scene, and co-operated with journalists only as much as was strictly necessary. Niven observed of her that 'she was wise enough, and had the inbred common sense, to spot the phonies who were clustered around her'.

Gigi opened at Broadway's Fulton Theater on 24 November 1951 after a try-out in Philadelphia. Gilbert Miller held few hopes for its success and, indeed, critical reaction to the play itself was lukewarm. For Audrey Hepburn, however, *Gigi* was a triumph. The hardened and hypercritical *Philadelphia Inquirer* had pronounced that she gave 'a wonderfully buoyant performance which establishes her as an actress of the first rank'.

The Broadway gurus were, if anything, even more enthusiastic. Brooks Atkinson in the *New York Times*, who found the play 'very trivial and old-fashioned', commented, 'Among other things it introduces us to Audrey Hepburn, a young actress of charm, honesty and talent who ought to be interned in America and trapped into appearing in a fine play.' Walter Kerr found 'Miss Hepburn . . . as fresh and frisky as a puppy out of a tub. She brings a candid innocence and a tomboy intelligence to a part that might have gone sticky, and her performance comes like a breath of fresh air in a stifling season.' He added, 'If the company as a whole had Miss Hepburn's *fundamental honesty of approach* [my italics], *Gigi* might be a thorough delight.' And William Hawkins of the *World Telegram and Sun* considered that Audrey had 'unquestionable beauty and talent'.

The world's love affair with Audrey Hepburn had begun. One week after the opening of *Gigi*, with the gracious consent of the cast's senior member, Cathleen Nesbitt, the marquee signs at the Fulton Theater were changed from 'GIGI with Audrey Hepburn' to 'AUDREY HEPBURN in GIGI'.

A few years later, Audrey's name as well as her face would promote Lux soap. Here, as the Lacto-Calamine girl, she was still anonymous.

WILLY, BILLY, BILL AND MEL

Roman Holiday: reporter Joe Bradley (Gregory Peck) introduces himself to the girl he has rescued from a street bench.

4

I still have this same goal: to be a great actress

AUDREY HEPBURN

Not since Garbo has there been anything like her, with the possible exception of Ingrid Bergman. After so many drive-in waitresses in movies, here is class

BILLY WILDER

It was Audrey Hepburn's ironic good fortune to work, in the course of seventeen films, with five of Hollywood's vintage big-league directors. Ironic because all of them had already done the work for which they will be remembered, even to some extent the great Billy Wilder; and, in the case of George Cukor, the irony was a bitter one, for in his hands she might well have scaled the heights of 'great' screen acting to which she aspired while never quite believing that her talent could achieve that goal. As it was, she was to achieve only part-success in the last of his major films, *My Fair Lady*.

It was under the guidance of William Wyler – stylist, master craftsman, doyen of the highest quality of 'middle-class' film, and relentless task-master – that the fledgling Audrey left the nest. Wyler's directing career had begun during the silent era. His first solo effort was in 1925 and, in the subsequent quarter of a century, he had proved his versatility and his box-office acumen with a canon of films that included *Counsellor at Law* (1933), *Dodsworth* (1936), *Wuthering Heights* (1939), *Mrs Miniver* (1942), and his masterpiece, *The Best Years of Our Lives* (1946).

Now, the director who had so successfully contributed to the careers of such heavyweight dramatic actresses as Bette Davis, Olivia de Havilland and the 'other' Hepburn, was to undergo a sea-change.

In his long career, Wyler had been tied to America and to studio stages. *Roman Holiday*, which he insisted on shooting in Rome itself, therefore marked a dramatic departure for him. Ian McLellan Hunter's short story had been around for a long time, part of an abandoned library of material earmarked by Frank Capra some years previously. The story is an unashamedly romantic and bitter-sweet account of twenty-four hours in the life of a young princess from an unspecified European monarchy who is on a series of state visits.

While in Rome, she rebels against the constraints of her royal existence and goes AWOL, sneaking out of the palace late one night. Unfortunately, the effects of a prescribed sleeping draft she has taken at bedtime soon overcome her and she falls asleep on a city bench. In the early hours of the morning she is found, drowsy and disoriented, by a handsome American news reporter. He soon realises her true identity and, scenting a major scoop, offers to show her the sights of Rome and arranges for a photographer friend to shadow them during their sightseeing. In the course of the day, he falls under her spell and finally abandons all thoughts of betraying her secret escapade. Controlled by Wyler's mastery, in monochrome travelogue settings, Hepburn and Gregory Peck turn this simple story into pure magic. As Wyler's biographer, Axel Madsen, puts it, 'Who would think a romantic comedy could have an unhappy ending? Wyler's happiest film is a fairy tale where, for once, the shepherd doesn't marry the princess.'

However, it took Wyler some time to realise the project. At first Paramount balked at the idea of location shooting in Italy, but Wyler stood his ground and finally won the argument. It then took all his powers of persuasion to get Gregory Peck to agree to play the role of reporter Joe Bradley when the actor, having read the script, saw that the real starring role belonged to the girl.

That left the problem of who was to play the girl. The studio had earmarked English actress Jean Simmons, with Elizabeth Taylor in mind as a possible alternative, but both actresses proved unavailable. At that point Wyler insisted on a non-American unknown for the role of Princess Anne: 'I wanted someone you could *believe* was brought up as a princess. That was the main

Left: Princess Anne, at a reception in Rome, has slipped her shoe off – to the dismay of the elderly dignitaries.

Opposite: With her fiancé James (later Lord) Hanson in 1952.

requirement, besides acting, looks and personality.' A search was instituted and thus it was that Hepburn's now famous screen test, directed by Thorold Dickinson, came to be made in England. On Wyler's instructions, the cameras were left running after the call of 'cut', and the result was sensational.

As Wyler himself described it, 'She jumped up in bed, relaxed now, and asked, "How was it? Was I any good?" She looked and saw that everybody was so quiet and that the lights were still on. Suddenly she realised the camera was still running and we got *that*

reaction too. Acting, looks, and personality! She was absolutely enchanting and we said, "That's the girl!" The test became sort of famous and was once shown on TV.'

Wyler's own accounts, however, tend to be uncomplicated regarding everything to do with the project. Certainly, the studio executives were enchanted but, in the Hollywood way, remained nervous about using a total unknown of limited experience. It was only after *Gigi* had opened, making Audrey the darling of Broadway, that they gave the go-ahead. Audrey, was, however, contracted to a tour of *Gigi* after the Broadway run, a problem that was finally solved by an agreement between Paramount and the producers that she could make the film before commencing the tour.

Signed at a fee of $12,500, and once again postponing plans for her marriage to the loyal and long-suffering James Hanson, Hepburn left for Rome and a baptism of what seemed literally fire in the intense August heat. Once again, Wyler's memories of the period are oversimplified. For him it was a case of the company being one big happy family, having a wonderful time amidst the architectural glories of the city, with the director relishing the fluidity of location work. And, indeed, the respect and affection that prevailed among the protagonists *did* make for a happy shoot, with Peck, famously, contacting his agent to insist that Audrey be given equal billing. It was a well-judged generosity on the part of a mega-star, and the beginning of a lifelong friendship throughout which Peck remained devoted to his one-time leading lady.

Their friendship and excellent working relationship also gave Hepburn her first taste of gossip-mongering. Rumours of an affair sprang up and refused to die for

JAMES HANSON - 1952

quite some time afterwards. Despite the fact that there was no truth in them, they placed an additional strain on her increasingly tenuous relationship with her fiancé. Hounded by the press, Audrey responded with the dignity and discretion that would characterise every public utterance for the rest of her life: always polite, always gracious, but direct,

simple and giving no quarter. And although, over the years, she was unable to avoid being the object of rumour, it was more often than not a matter of speculation rather than hard gossip. While she was unable actually to silence the press or banish the *paparazzi*, the quality of her personality seemed to elicit a collective decision to put the brakes on the more sensationalised aspects of reporting.

But if enthusiasm for the film was high, the mechanics of making it were something of an ordeal. As actors and crew threaded their way along the banks of the Tiber, in and out of sidewalk cafés, up and down the Spanish Steps and to set-ups that included the Forum, the Castel Sant' Angelo and the Colosseum, they had to contend with Roman traffic, Roman street sounds, and hordes of voluble and enthusiastic Roman spectators. Then Austrian cinematographer Franz Planer, later to become Audrey's chosen favourite, was replaced during filming. Some accounts say he was ill, others that the illness was a cover for a falling-out with Wyler. Fortunately for the film, his substitute was the splendid French cameraman Henri Alekan.

For Peck the difficulties of filming were compounded by the fact that he was in the throes of marital crisis. Although he, his wife Greta, and their sons were together in a rented villa for a good deal of the time, the couple would part soon after the completion of the film. A professional to his fingertips, and a gentleman, he did not allow his private problems to intrude on his work or to affect his seemingly effortless performance, which

marked a long-desired excursion into comedy.

But above all other problems, it was the heat – relentless, burning, stifling – that turned the summer months into a survival course. Make-up melted and ran down the actors' faces, requiring them to be washed down frequently; in the scene where Princess Anne awakes, the temperature in the palace boudoir rose to an intolerable 104 degrees, melting the candles in the wall brackets. For Audrey, thin, fragile, and accustomed to cooler northern climates, it was a nightmare. She, who could ill afford lack of nourishment, ate little. More often than not, shooting began at first light and continued through to midnight or beyond. Nothing, however, daunted Wyler, who, conditions and the fatigue of his stars nothwithstanding, wielded the whip in his usual manner, demanding take after take, sometimes as many as sixty in an afternoon.

It was a punishing schedule, but then Hepburn was already no stranger to flogging herself beyond the limits of her natural energy. She did everything required of her without a hint of complaint, again establishing a pattern of behaviour from which she would never deviate. Wyler, aware of her inexperience and her self-doubt in

Director William Wyler rehearses a scene with Audrey, who, as Anne, has had her hair cut in an act of rebellion. Peck and Eddie Albert, playing the photographer, look on.

carrying the burden of the central role, rewarded her with uncharacteristic expressions of praise and encouragement. He told writer Charles Higham that he set out to make Audrey 'be', rather than 'act', teaching her the fundamental of good screen acting, which is to communicate inner feeling rather than to play to the camera, an instrument that is sensitive to any artifice or untruth.

His efforts, coupled with Audrey's inner qualities, quick intelligence and hard work, paid off. When the director saw the rushes, he had 'that rare gut feeling that I was witnessing something very special indeed. She was a princess . . . But she was also every eager young girl who has ever come to Rome for the first time, and she reacted with so natural and spontaneous an eagerness that I, crusty veteran

that I was, felt tears in my eyes watching her . . . I knew that very soon the entire world would fall in love with her, as all of us on the picture did.'

The picture wrapped in September. Delays had resulted from the change of cameraman, and the film's by now thoroughly exhausted leading lady was left no respite before having to honour her commitment to Gilbert Miller's tour of *Gigi*. Unable to visit her fiancé in Toronto as she had wished, she came to realise that events had overtaken her and she was not ready for marriage. Despite Hanson's efforts to dissuade her, she put away the wedding dress that already hung in her wardrobe and cancelled the invitations already ordered. To the ill-concealed relief of the Baroness, on 15 December 1952 it was announced that 'The engagement between Mr James Hanson and Miss Audrey Hepburn has been broken.' Audrey subsequently issued a statement in which she said, 'When I get married, I want to be *really* married,' by which she meant she wished to be able to give herself and her time fully to the business of marriage.

Her views on the subject of marriage as a full-time occupation, a first call on one's loyalty and one's duty, never wavered. It was felt by those who knew her that when she married, it would have to be to somebody within, or close to, her now chosen profession.

Paramount executives were delighted with Hepburn, and although *Roman Holiday* had yet to be released, lost no time in lining up her next picture. The new vehicle was *Sabrina*, to be adapted to the screen from the Broadway play of the same name by Samuel Taylor. The story concerns Sabrina Fairchild, daughter of a dignified widower who is chauffeur to the multimillionaire Larrabee family on Long Island. The adolescent Sabrina develops a crush on the younger son, David, which even a post-adolescent spell in Paris fails to cure. She returns home, chic and *soignée*, and soon becomes the focus of romantic competition between David (despite the fact that he is engaged to be married) and his elder brother Linus, a confirmed bachelor and business tycoon. How the girl is got, and by whom, forms the stuff of this romantic trifle, which Audrey read and liked while passing briefly through New York *en route* to rejoining *Gigi*.

The picture was assigned to writer-director Billy Wilder, the German-born genius whose nominations and awards were

becoming too numerous to count. Acerbic, rude and outspoken, yet charming, erudite and exceptionally witty, Wilder had had a colourful life and career, and his extraordinary achievements marked him as one of Hollywood's premier creative forces. He had, with his long-time collaborator, Charles Brackett, written *Ninotchka* for Garbo and another great director, Ernst Lubitsch; he had made a batch of superior and memorable films including *Double Indemnity*, *The Lost Weekend*, *A Foreign Affair* and *Sunset Boulevard*; and two more superb films, *Some Like It Hot* and *The Apartment*, were still to come. All of this would ensure Wilder's immortality. If *Sabrina* remains one of his more inconsequential, albeit charming, achievements, it was significant in consolidating Audrey Hepburn's star status.

While preparations for the film were going on in Hollywood, Audrey was undergoing the gruelling task of taking *Gigi* on the road. The queen of Hollywood's costume designers, Edith Head, under contract to Paramount, the most style-conscious of studios, had dressed Hepburn for *Roman Holiday*, and was to do so again for *Sabrina*. She flew to San Francisco during the last stages of the *Gigi* tour,

Right: Audrey with Edith Head, the multiple-Oscar-winning queen of Hollywood studio costume designers.

Opposite: William Wyler (right), who launched Audrey's film stardom, and Billy Wilder, who consolidated it, with their protégée on the set of *Sabrina*.

strengthening an ideal working relationship with Audrey. Both cared deeply about the task in hand, both were bursting with creative ideas, both were disciplined perfectionists. Their long discussions and spirited shopping trips were pleasurable experiences, although, according to Charles Higham, the older woman was somewhat alarmed by the younger one's penchant for

consuming vast quantities of pastries and chocolates. The chocolates in particular would remain a passion, a self-confessed compensation for the years of wartime deprivation.

But an autocratic decision of Wilder's cast a shadow on Miss Head's plans. Edith Head, he announced, was to design the 'Cinderella' clothes worn by the young girl Sabrina before she leaves for Paris. The wardrobe with which she returns, however, was to be created by a rising young Parisian couturier, Hubert de Givenchy. The director had Hepburn flown to Paris to meet the elegant, handsome, six-foot-six-tall designer. Wilder's brainwave was to provide an identifying hallmark to Audrey Hepburn's image, both on the screen and off, for the rest of her days. It was undoubtedly her close association with Givenchy (who became one of her most loved and trusted friends) that, combined with her innate good taste and sense of style, elevated her to the ranks of the World's Best Dressed lists on numerous occasions. In an interview in later years, she said, 'I depend on Givenchy in the same way that American women depend on their psychiatrists.' A coda to these events must have gone some way to easing Edith Head's understandable disappointment: she was to receive the Best Costume Oscar for *Sabrina* – awarded, however, on the basis of two of Givenchy's gowns. The Frenchman gracefully refrained from making so much as a murmur.

Like Audrey, Givenchy was of aristocratic lineage – a count in his own right. Having abandoned law studies in favour of fashion design, by the age of twenty-six he had worked for all the leading fashion houses of Paris, including Jacques Fath and Schiaparelli, before acquiring his own salon on the Avenue George V. The story goes that, when Audrey presented herself, young, feminine, gamine, a startled Givenchy had to reorder his thoughts somewhat – he had been expecting *Katharine Hepburn*. Rapport and mutual respect between actress and designer were quickly established; his austere, classical lines and preference for simple subdued colours were perfectly in tune with Audrey's own simplicity of taste; and her thin, boyish, angular body was the ideal shape for his creations.

The filming of *Sabrina* marked

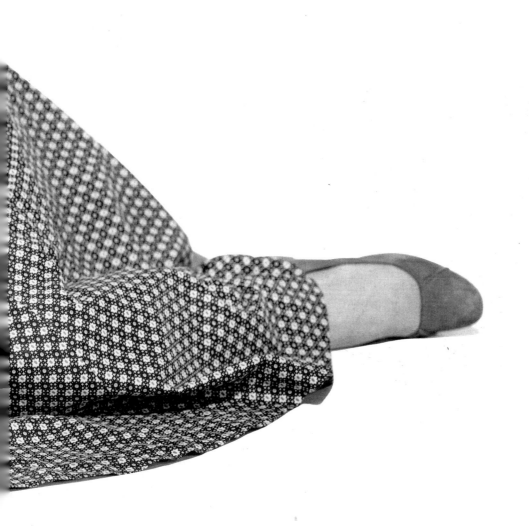

Linus Larrabee
(Humphrey Bogart) is
unaccustomed to
playing romantic
escort – especially to
Sabrina Fairchild, the
chauffeur's daughter.

another important first for
Audrey, that of working in a
Hollywood film studio. The
casting of the Larrabee brothers
had been finalised only after all
efforts to get Cary Grant had
failed. The feckless, irresponsible
womaniser, David, was to be
played by William Holden; the
crusty, bowler-hatted bachelor,
Linus, by Humphrey Bogart. It is
to the credit of all concerned that
the soufflé rose, for filming was
not a happy experience, and
Audrey's ability to keep her cool
was tested to the full.

The cause of tension was
Humphrey Bogart, a complex
man well known for his drinking
and Jekyll-and-Hyde personality.

This time he was all Hyde. He
had just completed *The Caine
Mutiny* and, despite his idyllically
happy marriage (his fourth) to
Lauren Bacall, appeared still to be
living in the skin of the paranoid
Captain Queeg. Commentators
have endlessly theorised about the
causes of his antagonism to the
script, the director and his co-
stars: his resentment that Cary
Grant had been first choice for the
role of Linus Larrabee; that
Audrey Hepburn was, in his view,
an inexperienced upstart; that
Holden and Wilder, who had made
the monumentally successful
Stalag 17 together, were close
friends.

Whatever the explanation, the
facts of his behaviour have never
been in dispute. Quick to needle

and hurl insults when thwarted,
Bogart met his match in Wilder,
whose German accent he mocked
and whom he called, among other
things, a 'Nazi son of a bitch' and
a 'kraut bastard'. According to
Wilder's biographer, Maurice
Zolotow, on one occasion the
Jewish-born Billy responded to
this form of abuse by looking
Bogie over slowly and saying, 'I
examine your face, Bogie, I look
at the valleys, the crevices, and
the pits of your ugly face – and I
know that somewhere underneath
the sickening face of a shit – is a
real shit.'

Bogie convinced himself that
the others were locked in some
sort of conspiracy against him, an
impression underlined by his
exclusion from the get-togethers at
the end of a day's work. Audrey
Wilder, Billy's wife, had this to
say: 'Bogie was forbidden access to
the regular after-hours drinks we
all enjoyed together. The reason
was, we just didn't think he was
fun to be with. Excluded,
ostracized, he reacted with anger
and became worse than ever. This
caused extreme tension on the
picture.'

He began giving interviews to
the press, in which he made his
feelings known in comments as
unjust as they were venomous. He
denigrated Audrey as a non-talent
who was just about okay if you

didn't mind at least twelve takes for every scene; he was at daggers drawn with Holden; and he put the seal on lifelong enmity with Wilder when he told *Time* magazine, 'Wilder is the kind of Prussian German with a riding crop. He's the type of director I don't like to work with. This picture *Sabrina* is a crock of shit anyway.'

But if Bogart's behaviour was the leitmotif of the summer of 1953, there were several other problems. Wilder, collaborating with Ernest Lehmann on the screenplay, was writing behind schedule, necessitating his use of delaying tactics in production which led, in turn, to the set-ups getting tied into all kinds of knots; in addition, as a chronic sufferer from back ailments, he was in extreme pain a good deal of the time.

Then there was Bill Holden. Warm, generous, fundamentally decent and long-married (his wife, Ardis, was known on the screen as Brenda Marshall), he was also a troubled man, riddled with insecurities and neuroses. Hypochondriac, chain-smoker, heavy drinker, a victim of ulcers and worried about his sexual adequacy, he fell head over heels in love with Audrey Hepburn, eleven years his junior, and – it is on record – remained in love with

her for the rest of his life. His physical presence was undeniably attractive, exuding a kind of macho reassurance to which Audrey, in turn, was responsive. But whatever transpired between them, the twenty-four-year-old Hepburn was not a candidate for the post of home-wrecker and, besides, was far too acute to imagine that marriage to Holden, which he desired, would be appropriate. If she ever did have any ideas of making a commitment to the relationship, they would in any case have been halted by Bill's confession that he had had a vasectomy. To have a child was Audrey's greatest desire.

Somehow, she managed to rise above this conglomeration of difficulties, ignoring Bogart's insults and dealing in private with

whatever emotions were being stirred by Holden. She gave a glorious performance, rich in that sense of wonder that she was peerless in conveying; as Sabrina she blossoms from scrawny teenager into svelte young woman, awakening from deluded dreams to the reality of love, with all the captivating charm and touching vulnerability that had been revealed in *Roman Holiday*.

She was enormously helped by Wilder, who quickly became her friend and mentor. He even gave her a bicycle on which she happily cycled her way round the sets and locations. A newcomer to the Hollywood jungle, she managed to skirt its dangers, spending her weekends mostly alone in her small rented apartment. In an interview the following year she said, 'I must be alone a lot. I'd be perfectly happy to be on my own from Saturday evening till Monday morning. It's my only chance to refuel.' Which is precisely what she did during the filming at Paramount – stay at home, listen to music (her tastes ranged wide, from jazz to opera), and cook simple meals for herself.

Filming moved to locations on Long Island, where Wilder used the actual estate of Paramount executive Barney Balaban for the Larrabee home. The shoot finally wrapped in August. It is reasonable to assume that, other than a lovesick Bill Holden, nobody was sorry to see the back of production.

In late August 1953, Audrey Hepburn flew back 'home' to London, her mother, and the British première of *Roman Holiday*. The film had already previewed to the trade papers and *Variety*, established bible of the industry, had declared it 'a winner' on all counts. Of its female star, the critic pronounced that she 'has talent, plus a personality that wears well on film . . . a delightful affectation in voice and delivery that is controlled just enough to have charm and serve as a trademark, as well as the looks and poise to make her role of a princess come over strongly.'

This was the first of many such accolades. On the film's release in the States, A. H. Weiler of the *New York Times* considered the relative newcomer to films 'a slender, elfin and wistful beauty, alternately regal and childlike in her profound appreciation of newly-found simple pleasures, and love'.

Thus began the journalists' Hepburn lexicon which persisted throughout her career. To charm, poise, elfin and wistful, add ethereal, urchin, style, chic, beauty, gazelle-like and, most popular of all, 'class' and gamine. Viewed almost forty years later, *Roman Holiday* retains its charm, its humour and its magic. It is obvious to all but the most curmudgeonly that in Hepburn the cinema had found a new ideal of female loveliness, a personality of unique attraction that would be much imitated, and much extolled the world over by everybody from the girls in the typing pool to the guru in such matters, Cecil Beaton.

Testimony to the influence of the Hepburn look – her slender elegance, her stylishness – was the effect it had on the greatest opera singer of the twentieth century, Maria Callas. After seeing *Roman Holiday*, the then generously proportioned *diva* resolved to lose weight and model herself on Audrey Hepburn. Photographs of

Callas after she had shed her weight clearly show the influence, even to the style of her clothes and hats.

The 'elfin and wistful' object of this emulation continued to assert that her face was too wide and her teeth crooked, that she didn't have much in the way of looks, and she couldn't *really* act, although she was trying her best to learn. She was, however, absolutely delighted with her reception on both sides of the Atlantic.

In all the words spoken by, and written about, her, it is evident that Hepburn's modesty in acknowledging her natural gifts was absolutely genuine. Under the poised, cool exterior and the iron will to succeed lurked a bundle of nerves and insecurities, a jittery disposition, as well as a warm and compassionate heart, a sharp mind and an infectious sense of humour. What set her apart from many actors of whom the same might be said was her ability to live alone with her emotional disabilities; she never allowed them to affect her public or professional behaviour, never took refuge in drugs or drink or promiscuity. She herself would have held this to be her good fortune, rather than something to admire.

During a brief visit she made to London in 1953, months before *Roman Holiday* was released, the word on Audrey was already out and she was much sought after by the press who considered her a 'British' success story. In an interview with Paul Holt of *Picturegoer* (whose annual award she would win at the end of that year) she said, of the attention she was attracting, 'This is the most trying time of my life. Just now I am no more than a publicity star. I have been made by writers. But what they have made me into is a shadow. I cannot become a substance until the public gives its approval.'

She did not have long to wait. Audiences were ecstatic, although more so in Britain and Europe (and Japan, where she remained a favourite for decades – 'Perhaps I look Japanese,' she once commented with characteristic humour) than in the USA. Coming in the wake of HRH Princess Margaret's poignant, duty-before-love romance with Group Captain Peter Townsend, the film had a special resonance which English audiences and journalists, in particular, were quick to appreciate. But if *Roman Holiday* did less business than anticipated in America, it still made the Box Office Top Ten for 1953, was voted one of the *New York Times*'s annual Top Ten, and won Audrey that paper's Best Actress Award.

At a party to mark the London

Happy . . . Audrey and Mel Ferrer.

première, Gregory Peck introduced Audrey to a close friend of his, a tall, dark, moody man, a writer, director and actor who was a partner of Peck's in the La Jolla Playhouse in California. He was also a film actor of erratic success, best known at the time for his starring role opposite Hollywood's other gamine, Leslie Caron, in *Lili*. Thrice married (twice to the same wife), a father of four, and eleven years Audrey Hepburn's senior, Mel Ferrer was restless, cultivated and ambitious. Audrey had seen *Lili* more than once and was already an admirer of a man

who exuded a combination of macho protectiveness and sensitivity, who was well read, a linguist and a man of the theatre. The attraction was instant, unstated and mutual.

They subsequently dined together one evening. Audrey expressed interest in doing a play with Ferrer and invited him to let her know if he should ever come across something suitable. She then left for the States to do some post-production work on *Sabrina* while attempting to keep the seriously smitten William Holden at bay.

WAR AND PEACE

As Natasha in *War and Peace*, reunited with Andrei (Mel Ferrer) at his deathbed.

For me, the only things of interest are those linked to the heart

AUDREY HEPBURN

She has authentic charm. Most people simply have nice manners

ALFRED LUNT

Melchior Gaston Ferrer was born in New Jersey in 1917, the son of a Cuban-born surgeon and a prominent New York socialite. He abandoned his studies at Princeton to act in summer stock, after which he edited a small newspaper in Vermont and wrote a children's book. In 1938 he headed for Broadway and found work as a dancer in the chorus of a couple of musicals, making his acting début two years later.

With his brains and charm, Ferrer should, perhaps, have had a higher profile by the time he met Audrey, but he was cursed with a restless ambition that constantly drove him to seek fresh challenges. He had been most successful in radio, working his way up from disc jockey to producer-director of top-rated shows for NBC – this after his flirtation with Broadway, and a year-long battle with polio which left him with a shrivelled arm. By sheer force of will, he exercised it back to strength.

In 1945 the young jack of all trades turned his attention to film, directing a low-budget screen version of *The Girl of the Limberlost* for Columbia. He assisted John Ford on *The Fugitive*, and made his own screen acting début in 1949 in a now forgotten movie called *Lost Boundaries*. He had small roles in *Rancho Notorious* and

Scaramouche, before his breakthrough as the embittered, crippled fairground puppeteer in *Lili*. But that success did not bring him stardom – his long, spare frame, sober mien and haunted El Greco looks were not consonant with the Hollywood fashion in leading men and, from the end of the 1950s, his frequent film acting assignments and occasional forays into producing and directing took place mainly in Europe.

Ferrer took seriously Audrey's expression of interest in doing a play with him. Shortly after their meeting he had read (in the original French) Jean Giraudoux's *Ondine*, a play which had originally been performed in Paris in 1939 to rapturous acclaim. In 1961 it would receive a first-class production in England, directed by Peter (now Sir Peter) Hall, starring his then wife, Leslie Caron; and in 1962 one of Audrey's heroes, Sir Frederick Ashton, created the ballet version for Dame Margot Fonteyn at Covent Garden.

Ondine is a romantic fable, based on medieval legend, in which a knight-errant falls in love with a water sprite. Unable to deal with her innocence, he betrays her; he is punished with death, while she escapes back to the amorphous world from which

she came. Ferrer immediately recognised the play as a perfect vehicle for Audrey's delicate, other-worldly qualities and saw an opportunity for himself in the role of Hans the knight. Audrey's reaction was similar, and Ferrer went ahead with plans.

Although *Ondine* was hardly the stuff of which Broadway successes were usually made, with Hepburn willing to star in it the Playwrights' Company was more than willing to risk a production. The distinguished dramatist Robert E. Sherwood was to supervise the production, and invited his long-time colleague Alfred Lunt to direct. Audrey had met the Lunts briefly in their dressing room after a performance in London, and shared in the general admiration in which they were held.

American actor-director Alfred Lunt and his British wife Lynn Fontanne were the undisputed king and queen of Broadway and of London's West End, far eclipsing even the Oliviers as a husband-and-wife team. Legendarily inseparable both personally and professionally, they pursued their craft with an almost insane passion, absolute perfectionism and awesome expertise. *Ondine* was one of the rare projects in which Lynn Fontanne was not involved –

officially, that is. During rehearsals, she was very much a presence, observing, and from time to time intervening to help directly with the finer detail of a performance.

Delighted with the casting of Audrey, the producers were less confident about Mel. But the package was Mel's and they had no alternative. A member of the production team later remarked, 'We bought Hepburn and the price was Ferrer. It turned out to be much too expensive.' Whether or not anybody foresaw the difficulties that Mel's insecure ego and arrogant manner would create, the unfortunate Alfred Lunt came to bear the full brunt, while Audrey remained seemingly oblivious of Ferrer's tantrums.

By the time rehearsals were under way in December 1953, she was totally in love with Mel. They spent every moment of their leisure time together, giving rise to animated gossip and endless speculation. Having, as she believed, finally found the right man to love and protect her, Audrey appeared to lose all objectivity where Mel was concerned. It was to become her habit with the men in her life: she chose not to acknowledge their negative actions and always to defend them, even when their

behaviour was clearly detrimental to her own well-being.

Alfred Lunt was a relentless task-master, and rehearsals for this difficult play were very taxing, made more so by the tensions that developed between the director and Ferrer. Mel's attitude to Lunt's ideas was patronising, and he made complaints to the producers about Lynn Fontanne's involvement, which he viewed as interference. Moody and temperamental, he tried to push suggestions that would remove some of the focus from Audrey on to him.

The play opened its pre-Broadway try-out in Boston on 29 January 1954 and was very well received, but the reception accorded his beloved Audrey seemed to spark off further dissatisfaction in Mel. He was openly disparaging about Lunt's production, and made fresh demands to the Playwrights' Company that the adapter, Maurice Valency, should do some rewriting to expand the role of Hans. An outraged Sherwood protested to Ferrer's agent, who in turn advised Mel to change his attitude. He apologised to Lunt, but the backbiting had finally and obviously affected Audrey.

According to the Lunts' biographer, Jared Brown, her confidence in her own performance

had been undermined and she was finding it difficult being in the middle of the conflicts between her future husband and her director. She flew from Boston to see Robert Sherwood, and suggested that it might be best for everybody if she were to leave the production – an unthinkable proposal in Sherwood's opinion. After much discussion, he managed to reinstate her belief in herself and in the production. He wired Lunt: '. . . I have had a very useful and sensible talk with Audrey Hepburn . . . Audrey said to me that she could ask nothing better for her future career than always to be directed by you and I take that statement literally as evidence of her intelligence.'

The Boston papers raved about the play and about Audrey, who in an interview with the *Boston Globe* said, 'We are fortunate to have Mr Lunt as director. I have

Mel and Audrey as
Hans the knight and
Ondine.

never met a man whose
encouragement, kindness and
understanding does so much for an
actress. Miss Fontanne, with her
enormous experience, is always
ready to give an actor advice
when we go to her.'

On 18 February 1954, *Ondine*
opened at New York's 46th Street
Theater. Audrey was dressed by
the Russian-born designer
Valentina. The star's appearance
in a scanty costume made of
delicate green fishnet and some
strands of 'seaweed' caused a
sensation. The virginal Gigi and
the unsullied Princess Anne of
Roman Holiday was now a near-
nude nymph of unquestionably
erotic appeal – and even the
puritanically-minded among the
audience were bewitched. An
executive from Paramount
commented, 'Any other actress
would have been censored from
here to Timbuctoo for this Minsky

outfit. But what censor would
dare point a finger at Audrey
Hepburn?'

The hardened New York critics,
who had fallen in love with Gigi
two years previously, were
transported into ecstasies by
Ondine. Brooks Atkinson
considered the production 'ideal
from every point of view' and
Audrey's performance 'all grace
and enchantment, disciplined by
an instinct for the realities of the
theater'. Atkinson also thought
Mel Ferrer 'the perfect
counterpart'. Some critics were
lukewarm about the play itself; all
were captivated by the leading
lady, but Richard Watts Jr of the
New York Post stated that his
'only reservation has to do with
the performance of Mel Ferrer as
the knight-errant . . . To my
mind, his playing is curiously
uninteresting. It lacks vividness,
style and imagination almost
completely, which is all the more
distracting because these are the
qualities that the production of

Ondine possesses so winningly.'
Eric Bentley, who disliked the
evening but for Audrey, went
further, virtually blaming all the
deficiencies, as he saw them, on
Mel.

Despite the success of the show,
his apology to Lunt, and the fact
that he was engaged to be married
to Audrey, whom he clearly
adored, the hapless Mel found it
impossible to kneel to her
triumph. He continued to niggle,
and demanded that he share all of
Audrey's curtain calls, depriving
her of a solo bow. This particular
aspect of his behaviour gave rise
to much unpleasant talk and
aroused hostility towards a man
whom many considered charming.
According to Jared Brown, a
naïve woman at the opening-night
party asked Alfred Lunt, 'Did you
learn anything from working with
a movie star like Mel Ferrer?' The
dumbstruck director replied, 'Yes
madam. I learned that you cannot
make a knight-errant out of a
horse's ass.'

With Mel in *Ondine*.

influence over her daughter was a challenge to her own.

Audrey, caught yet again in the conflict between two opposing forces, was under a lot of strain. She was also finding eight performances a week of *Ondine* exhausting, and had to cope with the additional burden of a constant stream of journalists eager to blazon the details of her romance with Ferrer across their pages. After the performance on 25 March 1954, she attended the New York end of the annual Academy Awards ceremony, which was held at the Center Theater. Still in her costume, and accompanied by her mother and her fiancé, she was rushed to the venue in a Rolls-Royce with police motorcycle escort. Once there, she changed into a waiting Givenchy gown, making it to her seat just in time for the Best Actress announcement. Apart from Audrey, the nominees for 1953 were Leslie Caron for *Lili*, Ava Gardner for *Mogambo*, Deborah Kerr for *From Here to Eternity* and the soon-to-be-forgotten Maggie McNamara for *The Moon Is Blue*. Despite the fact that the gracious Englishwoman, the lovely Deborah Kerr, was considered by many in the movie industry to be the strongest contender, the only real surprise at Audrey's win came from the recipient herself.

Several of Audrey's friends, including Cathleen Nesbitt and the prominent columnist Radie Harris, who had first introduced her to the Lunts in London, looked with foreboding on Audrey's association with Mel, but nobody was more bitterly opposed to it than Baroness Van Heemstra. Mel's first marriage to Frances Pilchard, the mother of his first two children, had ended in divorce. He had then married Barbara Tripp, had two more children, and been through another divorce. The bonds with Frances were, however, strong, and the couple had remarried. When Mel met Audrey, Frances was his wife but the relationship was again showing signs of strain. When word reached her that her husband was showing more than a passing interest in his leading-lady-to-be, she divorced him for the second time. Ella Van Heemstra, choosing to overlook her own marital history, considered Ferrer a dubious prospect, but it is reasonable to speculate that she was also suffering from having to confront somebody whose strong

Totally flustered, she made her way on to the podium and proceeded to take a turn in the wrong direction, landing up in the wings. She made her way back to affectionate laughter from the audience, and accepted her Oscar with the usual obligatory expressions of gratitude to many people. She went on to say, 'I mustn't allow this award to turn my head or persuade me to forget my life's ambition – to become a truly great actress.'

For all her genuine modesty, the new star was fast learning the language of fame. Within the Hollywood community, there were those who suffered a flash of jealousy and resentment at Audrey's swift rise; and there were a handful of sceptics. Even Don Hartman, production chief at Paramount, which stood to gain most from the success of *Roman Holiday*, said a day or two after the Oscar ceremony, 'The question which has to be answered is, can she hold up a picture on her own?' The British critic Milton Shulman spoke for several when he aired the view that 'Except for this ability to exude an impish, waif-like quality, there is no evidence that Audrey Hepburn can do anything else.'

A few days later, she won the coveted Tony Award for Best Actress for her performance in *Ondine*. This was a double that had been achieved by only one other actress – Shirley Booth, the previous year. If Audrey was amazed and overwhelmed by the degree of her success, she was also elated. Now the highest-paid actress on Broadway, at $2,500 per week plus a percentage, and with Paramount Pictures attempting to buy out her Associated British Pictures contract for a then unprecedented million dollars, she was truly the world's darling, poised to marry the first man with whom she had fallen unconditionally in love.

By April of that year, however, her anaemia was worsening and she was on the edge of nervous exhaustion. It became clear that she could not continue with *Ondine* indefinitely. The play duly closed at the end of June and, at her doctor's suggestion, the far-from-well actress left for Switzerland to recuperate. She had worked without respite, and in often difficult circumstances, since arriving in New York for the rehearsals of *Gigi* in October 1951. She had changed direction, lost one fiancé and found another, and been catapulted to stardom. It was not surprising that her highly-strung nature and frail constitution had finally called a halt.

Mel flew to Italy where he was to film *La Madre* for an Italian company. He and Audrey planned to marry later in the year and he had arranged advance permission to be absent from filming for a few days. She, meanwhile, was making her way in a chauffeur-driven limousine to the fashionable Swiss resort of Gstaad. *En route*, she was overcome with exhaustion and felt unwell. Her chauffeur suggested they take a detour and stop at the Burgenstock, a spectacularly beautiful and exclusive retreat in the mountains, three thousand feet above, and overlooking, Lake Lucerne. Audrey lunched at the exquisite Grand Hotel and met the owner, Fritz Frey, an urbane and sympathetic man and a renowned hotelier, with whom she found an immediate rapport. His family had created the 500-acre Burgenstock, with its three splendid hotels, its beautiful park, a funicular railway, and even its own police to protect the place and its distinguished visitors from intrusion.

After lunch, Audrey resumed her drive to Gstaad. It proved the worst possible choice of destination. A resort frequented by jet-setters and gawping tourists, it was the opposite of secluded and quiet. An indiscreet member of staff at the Palace Hotel had put the word about that she was arriving, and she drove straight into a waiting posse of reporters and photographers, who bombarded her with questions about herself, her career and, most difficult of all, Mel. In a state of barely suppressed hysteria, she telephoned her new friend Fritz Frey, and ordered her chauffeur to take the long drive back to Burgenstock.

Frey and his wife leased Audrey a secluded chalet, small, attractively modern, comfortable, and situated in idyllic surroundings. Her poor condition was obvious to the Freys, who devoted themselves to protecting her privacy and seeing that all her needs were met. It was a haven of peace and beauty. Audrey passed the days resting, walking, eating the delicious fresh produce, and talking to Mel in Italy as often as they could reach each other on the long-distance telephone between the mountain outpost and his film location in Sardinia.

In these ideal conditions, she gradually came back to life and began to make wedding plans. After a civil marriage conducted in the mayor's parlour at Burgenstock on 24 September, the couple were married by Pastor Endiguer in the little chapel on 25 September 1954. Despite driving mountain rain and her mother's tears, Audrey had never been

Mr and Mrs Mel Ferrer leave the church in Burgenstock after their wedding ceremony on 25 September 1954.

happier. Dressed in a simple but ravishing Givenchy dress with matching white hat and veil, and carrying a small bouquet of lilies of the valley and tiny roses, she was given away by Sir Neville Bland, a close friend of Ella Van Heemstra's and a former British Ambassador to the Netherlands. Two of Mel's children were among the twenty-five guests who attended the simple ceremony, at which press attendance was kept to a bare minimum. After the reception at the country club, Mel and Audrey left to spend a few

days secretly in Switzerland before leaving for Italy.

The Ferrers spent a month in Italy while Mel completed his work on *La Madre*. He had found a beautiful restored farmhouse in the Alban Hills outside Rome. Surrounded by grapevines and boasting a glorious view and lovely gardens, the granite and stucco house also had a huge traditional Italian farmhouse kitchen in which Audrey could potter and cook pasta to her heart's content. Best of all, the estate was shared with a few dogs, several cats, a donkey and a pair of doves. Audrey was blissfully happy, and determined to stay that way. She was terrified of repeating her mother's marital failures and inflicting a broken home on the children she longed to have. From the outset of marriage to Mel, she evolved a master plan which would allow her to put their relationship first by avoiding the damaging separations endemic in show-business marriages. Yet she had no thoughts of abandoning her career. Eighteen months after her marriage, in an interview with the London *Evening News*, she summed up the views from which she never deviated:

'I think marriage and art can develop together. The thing to remember is that you have to work at both . . . When I got married to Mel I decided that if I worked for, say, three months on my own career, I would save another three months for being a married woman and a proper wife. After all, Mel has his problems, too; and what sort of a marriage would it be if when he came home tired and wanting to talk about his problems, I was too tied up with my own ambitions to talk about anything but mine?'

In November 1956, she said, 'Whether we work together or not, we shall avoid long partings at all

costs. We haven't done so badly so far – only two months' separation all told in two years of marriage.' And Mel, forcibly echoing his wife's sentiments, told the London *Daily Express*, 'The only thing that I am adamant about is that Audrey and I should be able to be together. I do not mean that Audrey and I must work as a team in the same pictures – in fact, I think that would be a bad thing for her career. But I insist that we work beside each other – even if it is just in the same country.'

For the first couple of years, their lives followed a pattern that made it relatively easy for Audrey to live up to her ideals. She and Mel were both contracted to appear in Dino de Laurentiis's epic production of *War and Peace*, playing opposite one each other as Natasha and Prince Andrei. Shooting was scheduled to begin in the late winter, but plans were thrown into confusion when Audrey discovered she was pregnant. Absolutely delighted, she was willing to withdraw from the film, but since her name and her presence were considered vital, De Laurentiis undertook the monumental task of rescheduling the shoot for the late summer of 1955.

Meanwhile, Mel was to film *Oh Rosalinda!* at Elstree Studios just

outside London in the New Year. He was also desperately keen to sell the idea of a film version of *Ondine*, particularly with Audrey's stock riding high. *Sabrina* had been released in the USA in September to a very good critical reception. Bosley Crowther in the *New York Times* praised the film extravagantly, calling its star 'sweetly bewitching' and 'a young lady of extraordinary range of sensitive and moving expressions . . . even more luminous than she was as a princess last year, and no more than that can be said.' *Variety* thought that 'Miss Hepburn again demonstrates a winning talent for being "Miss Cinderella" and will have audiences rooting for her all the way.' The response to *Sabrina* was confirmed with yet another Best Actress Oscar nomination in the New Year. (Grace Kelly won, for *The Country Girl*.)

Early in the winter of 1954, Mel accompanied Audrey to Holland where she had agreed to make a number of fund-raising appearances for charity. By now, the Queen of Holland excepted, Audrey had become the most famous Dutchwoman in the world and she was greeted with something approaching mob hysteria. In Amsterdam, while she signed photographs at a department store, matters went

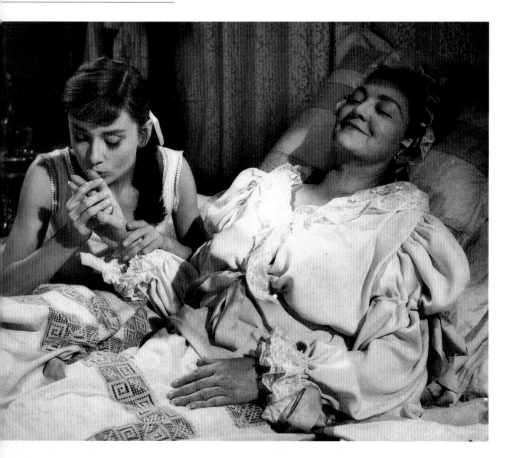

De Laurentiis rescheduled *War and Peace* yet again to start earlier than late July.

It was a massive undertaking: the domes of Moscow were convincingly reconstructed on the banks of the Tiber; other sets were housed in Rome's vast Cinecittà studios. De Laurentiis had hired 15,000 soldiers of the Italian army for whom authentic Russian period uniforms had to be made. With the changes of schedule, the Russian heavy-snow scenes had to be filmed in the summer heat, requiring large 'snow' machines which disgorged cornflakes dipped in gypsum. Italian muddles and inefficiency were to dog the production: once again, Audrey was to find herself with a gruelling task.

The filming of *War and Peace* had a curious history. By a strange coincidence of ideas, four producers – MGM, David O. Selznick, Mike Todd and Dino De Laurentiis – had all decided in 1954 to embark on a screen version of Tolstoy's epic. In each case, they had Audrey in mind to play Natasha, described in the novel thus: 'Dark-eyed with a wide mouth . . . full of life, with bare childish shoulders, which had risen out of her bodice in her rapid motion, her black curls tossed back, her slender bare arms . . . her bosom undeveloped . . . such

completely out of control. Police had to be called as the crowd smashed through the plate-glass windows in their desire to get a look at their idol. It was a deeply unhappy experience for Audrey, who at the best of times detested large crowds and always had an abhorrence of violence in any form.

The couple spent Christmas in Burgenstock, which was to be their only base for quite some time. On New Year's Day 1955 they left for London, where they had taken a comfortable flat in Portman Square. Much time and energy were given to wooing producers who might finance a film of *Ondine*, but nobody

believed it to be a suitable subject for the cinema and their efforts came to nothing. Audrey visited the set of *Oh Rosalinda!* and the rumours that Mel controlled her every move were fuelled when he objected to photographers at Elstree taking pictures of his wife.

Audrey returned to the Burgenstock to cosset herself in her pregnancy, but tragedy struck in March, when she suffered a miscarriage. It was an emotional trauma that left her with little interest in work, although she had read extensively to prepare herself for the role of Natasha. Mel, however, persuaded her that work would be the best therapy and, with the news of her misfortune, was Natasha with her wonder, her delight, her shyness.'

Selznick announced that he would hire Ben Hecht to write the screenplay; Todd actually contracted Robert E. Sherwood and director Fred Zinnemann. In the event, after much toing and froing, all but De Laurentiis dropped out of the race. He hired the veteran King Vidor to write the screenplay and direct the picture and, according to several accounts, including Mel Ferrer's own, signed the actor to play Prince Andrei quite some time before Audrey Hepburn was officially approached. This did not prevent the gloom merchants from suggesting that he had ridden into the picture on his wife's coat-tails.

Audrey was now a huge star with an eager public awaiting her next picture, and was able to drive a hard bargain. Her agent secured a salary reputed to have been $350,000, plus generous weekly expenses, and more to come if the shooting exceeded twelve weeks. When Franz Planer proved unavailable, she requested, and got, cinematographer Jack Cardiff, whose work she admired, and also asked for make-up man Alberto de Rossi (and his wife Grazia for her hair), thus beginning a long association which would influence her cosmetic style over the years. She had no say

Opposite: War and Peace: the young actress Natasha Rostov confides her dreams, hopes and fears to her mother (Lea Seidl).

Right: Natasha with Pierre (Henry Fonda).

over the casting – she never did, nor did she try to – and was given fifty-year-old Henry Fonda as Pierre, Natasha's most enduring love, thus continuing the tradition begun with *Roman Holiday* of pairing the childlike Audrey with men many years her senior.

In the spring of 1955, the Ferrers left for Rome to begin rehearsals and costume fittings. Audrey's desire to get every detail right had not deserted her, and she involved herself in

meticulously checking all her costumes to ensure period accuracy. She and Mel had managed to rent their wonderful honeymoon farmhouse again; the film company supplied a chauffeur-driven limousine to take them on the daily hour-long drive into the city. The distance was worth it – the jasmine and bougainvillea, the herb gardens and the flowers were blooming, and the house was a tranquil haven after the end of a long, and

Innocence.

Below: Prince Andrei Volkonsky is smitten with Natasha.

Seduced by the
corrupt Count Anatol
Kuragin (Vittorio
Gassman).

soon to be intolerably hot, day's filming.

The Texan-born director King Vidor had made his feature début in 1919 and was responsible for at least two major masterpieces of the silent era. *The Big Parade* (1925), an epic anti-war film, demonstrated his fluency with the big image, while the humanism and technical virtuosity of *The Crowd* (1928) confirmed his quality as a film-maker of considerable power. *Hallelujah!* (1929), one of the earliest talkies, *Street Scene* (1931) and *Our Daily Bread* (1934) were highlights of his work after the coming of sound, but his gifts seemed diluted by the subsequent commercial demands of the industry. *Duel in the Sun* (1947) was his last major success before he embarked on *War and Peace*.

Vidor himself wrote a vivid account of the filming of the battle scenes, which were fraught with difficulties but which turned out very well in the end. The sweep of the retreat from Moscow, led by Herbert Lom's Napoleon, was most impressive, but the three-and-a-half-hour narrative failed to gel. The intimate scenes lack bite, and the motley conglomeration of accents from a multinational cast strains credibility. Only Audrey, rising above the battles she constantly fought to keep reporters and voluble Italian visitors away from the set, while coping yet again with the Roman heat and the long hours, managed to elevate the limp script – the product ultimately of six writers, including Vidor, the English playwright Bridget Boland, and the Italian screenwriter Ivo Pirelli.

In his book *On Film Making*, written in 1972, Vidor had this to say about Hepburn: 'During the years since that film was made and several years before, no one has ever crossed my mind who could have so admirably suited the part. Audrey . . . moves through a scene with a rhythmic grace that is a director's delight.' The director, who had worked with a score of the best from Lillian Gish to Barbara Stanwyck (both of whom he revered), also writes of Audrey, 'Whenever I am asked that most embarrassing of questions – "Who is your favourite actress of all those you have directed?" – one always comes immediately to mind.'

That Audrey achieved a performance of convincing emotional range from so unhelpful a script and in such arduous circumstances finally provided proof for the doubters who felt she could do no more than be herself: waif-like and appealing, with a little French *haute-couture* chic thrown in for good measure. She hated working out of sequence, trying to retain a clear line of emotion over so long a period of time and in the face of constant changes to the schedule; she came the closest she ever would to throwing a tantrum about the constant intrusions of visitors to the set; and she was exhausted by her hard efforts to perfect her performance.

Mel Ferrer continued to play the protector of his wife, fuelling the rumours that he was Svengali to her Trilby. Certainly, there is little doubt that he was an assertive and controlling influence in Audrey's life, but it is equally true that she invited protection, and, at least in the early years of their marriage, was willing to be guided by him and, at times, even subservient to his wishes. Vidor himself countered rumours that Mel had been troublesome: 'It is not true that Ferrer interfered with the making of *War and Peace*. I had heard bad things about Mel, but I found him charming. He didn't try to direct the picture and we got on fine.

'I had the feeling that Audrey needed somebody like him to make her decisions for her. She's an innocent who doesn't know the business the way Mel does. He did all the talking for her. He knows what is right for her. He knows how much money she should be

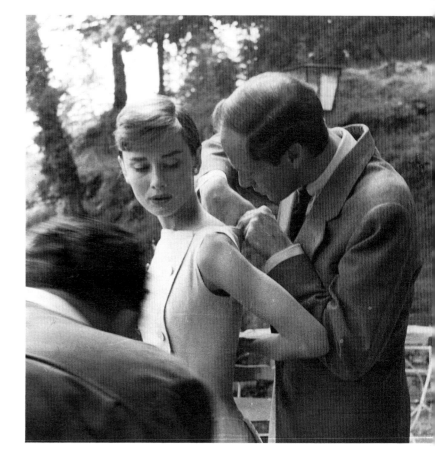

An attentive husband, photographed at Burgenstock.

getting, and he's a director himself so he understands whether she's getting a fair deal.'

So, he was asked by journalist Thomas Wiseman, were there no rows in Italy? Vidor replied, 'In Italy every conversation sounds like a row. I soon found out that unless you yell at the Italians you don't get anywhere. So I yelled. Henry Fonda also had to yell sometimes.' And Audrey? 'She let Mel do the yelling for her.'

Towards the end of filming, Audrey was approached by producer Hal B. Wallis to star in the film version of Tennessee Williams's drama *Summer and Smoke*. Wallis flew to Rome for discussions and found that Audrey

was, indeed, interested in playing Williams's sad, frustrated Mississippi spinster, but one can only be thankful that negotiations broke down. It is difficult to imagine Audrey Hepburn, aged twenty-six, with her elfin looks and quirky accent, in a role that was eventually played by a perfectly cast Geraldine Page.

But there were other offers. In October, fatigued and her nerves frayed from the long, hard months of *War and Peace*, Audrey, with her beloved Mel in tow, flew to Hollywood for discussions about a new film. If the complications surrounding the deal could be sorted out, she would have a new leading man, aged fifty-seven.

BONJOUR PAREE

Funny Face: the 'Empathicalist's' dance.

6

Who's to say I could really have been a dancer? But certainly dancing has stood me in good stead

AUDREY HEPBURN

Audrey . . . makes my soul fly. She opens me up to beautiful feelings

STANLEY DONEN

The genesis of Audrey's next film was complicated. The starting point was a musical, *Wedding Day*, that writer Leonard Gershe had intended for Broadway in 1951. But this show, with a score by Vernon Duke and lyrics by Ogden Nash, failed to get off the ground and eventually ended up in the hands of Roger Edens, one of MGM's top producers of musicals. Edens ditched the score in favour of a collection of Gershwin standards and changed the name to that of a Broadway show in which Fred Astaire and his sister Adele had appeared in 1927 – *Funny Face*.

Stanley Donen was signed to direct and Audrey, according to some accounts, was told that Fred Astaire had agreed to do the picture if she would consent to co-star with him. Astaire's own account is the reverse: Edens, he said in his autobiography, had told him that Audrey liked the script and had agreed to star, provided that Astaire played opposite her. In the event, each was thrilled about the other, but numerous complications bedevilled the project.

Warner Brothers held the rights to George and Ira Gershwin's songs, and would release them to MGM only in exchange for Stanley Donen's services on *The Pajama Game*. More seriously, Paramount were adamant that they were not lending Audrey to Metro, and were reluctant to release Astaire, with whom they had a two-picture deal. After protracted negotiations, it was agreed that Edens and his outfit would move over to Paramount and make the picture there.

As Astaire describes it, 'The dates conflicted; Paramount could not handle it; Metro could not swing it; it was hopeless. I was repeatedly told that there was no chance to put the deal across.

'However, I knew that Audrey wanted to make the picture and that sooner or later they would all come around – *because Audrey is a lady who gets her way* [my italics]. So, I just told my agents to forget all other projects for me. I was waiting for Audrey Hepburn. She asked for me, and I was ready.

'This could be the last and only opportunity I'd have to work with the great and lovely Audrey and I was not missing it. Period.'

These words, a tribute to Audrey from the greatest dancer – outside the world of classical ballet – of the twentieth century, are indicative of the extraordinary esteem in which Hepburn was held after only two movies (*War and Peace* had not yet been released), and the powerful leverage that esteem gave her.

Audrey and Mel arrived in Hollywood in October. As well as *Funny Face*, there had been talk of another picture, an adaptation of Claude Anet's French novel *Ariane* for Billy Wilder. This seemed an attractive proposition, but Wilder was overrunning on current commitments so plans were unable to proceed.

The Ferrers were engaged in discussions almost until Christmas, while Gershe, Edens and Donen worked on the original script, rewriting extensively and adding a couple of new songs. Meanwhile, Kay Thompson, a powerhouse nightclub performer and author of the successful *Eloise* books, was signed for the movie's other major role, that of Maggie, the hard-boiled, dynamic fashion editor. Joseph Casper, in his study of Stanley Donen, maintains that the character was modelled on Carmel Snow of *Harper's Bazaar*; Charles Higham has it that she is based on *Vogue*'s Diana Vreeland. It makes little difference. It's a great part, and Thompson, only an occasional movie performer, proved a superb choice.

Despite her desire to work with Astaire and her enthusiasm for the script, Audrey took some considerable time to commit to the picture. She was in a position to command a lot of money and lay down her own conditions and, if she was the most co-operative,

Left: On the set with Givenchy, who designed the clothes.

Opposite: On set during a break: Astaire, a proprietary Mel, Audrey in her 'Cinderella' clothes, and top American fashion model Dovima, who appears in the film.

attended to – Gladys de Segonzac, the wardrobe supervisor, said of Audrey that she 'could wear anything with taste and dignity. She can stand for hours at a time, never fidgets, never squirms. You know how tired she must be, but she never mentions it. She makes her changes with amazing rapidity, with never a wasted motion.'

Once again, Edith Head was the costume designer; once again, in terms of Audrey's clothes, she was left with the 'Cinderella' outfits, while the spectacular Paris ensembles were created by Givenchy.

Audrey was tired, but it was a happy time. She and Mel had rented director Anatole Litvak's attractive house on the beach at Malibu, and with only a five-day working week, she was able to recoup her strength and enjoy life at weekends.

After her preliminary work with Eugene Loring, Fred Astaire arrived to start rehearsals. Audrey, understandably, was very nervous, doubting her capacity to acquit herself well as a dancing partner to a living legend who, apart from his historic partnership with Ginger Rogers, had danced on screen with Eleanor Powell, Rita Hayworth, Judy Garland and Cyd Charisse.

Many years later, when Fred Astaire, aged eighty-two, was

charming, hard-working and undemanding of stars on the set, she was very tough in holding out for what she wanted. Eventually, her agent Kurt Frings concluded a satisfactory deal, but there remained the problem of what might possibly be too long a separation from Mel. He was due to work with Ingrid Bergman in Jean Renoir's *Elena et Ses Hommes* in Paris. The combined persuasion of Paramount and the other interested parties managed

to get his start date delayed so that Audrey and he would be in Paris at the same time.

With everything finally sorted out, Mel and Audrey returned to Switzerland to spend a quiet Christmas. Then it was back to California to begin preparations for the film, which at that stage meant taxing barre practice and extensive dance rehearsals with Eugene Loring, co-choreographer with Fred Astaire. There were also exhausting costume fittings to be honoured with a Life Achievement Award by the American Film Institute, Audrey, as was her generous habit, flew to Los Angeles to pay tribute to him. She described her first meeting with him thus: 'I remember he was wearing a yellow shirt, grey flannels, a red scarf knotted around his waist instead of a belt, and the famous feet were clad in soft moccasins and pink socks. He was also wearing that irresistible smile.'

She continued, 'One look at this most debonair, elegant and distinguished of legends and I could feel myself turn to solid lead, while my heart sank into my two left feet. Then suddenly I felt a hand around my waist, and with his inimitable grace and lightness, Fred literally swept me off my feet. I experienced the thrill that all women at some point in their lives have dreamed of — to dance just once with Fred Astaire.'

The story of *Funny Face* was inspired by Richard Avedon, one of America's most famous and gifted fashion photographers, who had trained one of his models and then married her. In the film, the fashion editor of 'Quality' magazine is looking for a new and 'different' face to promote as the 'Quality' woman, and model the new collection of a famous French designer. Her high-flying

photographer, Dick Avery, persuades her to use Jo Stockton, a Greenwich Village blue-stocking whom they encounter at her work in a musty Village bookshop.

The reluctant Jo is finally coerced into accepting the assignment because it carries a trip to Paris, where she hopes to meet her idol Professor Flostre, the philosopher founder of 'Empathicalism'.

In Paris, the world-weary Dick and the unworldly Jo fall in love. They come unstuck over Flostre, who is a lecherous *poseur*, but all is resolved in time for a happy ending. This simple romantic flim-flam parodies Existentialism and its followers, cocking a snook at

the counter-culture of the 1950s, and also affectionately satirises the world of high fashion.

Funny Face, the perfect vehicle for Audrey, was the first and last of her films to make full use of her dancing ability. It also called upon her to perform four immortal Gershwin songs, which she sang in a voice — low-pitched and unmistakably hers — whose very imperfections lend the numbers a wistful charm.

Principal photography began with interiors on the Paramount lot in April 1956. Richard Avedon had been hired as 'Special Visual Consultant' and, working closely with cinematographer Ray June and the inventive Donen,

'Bonjour Paree!' Kay
Thompson, Fred
Astaire and Audrey
Hepburn atop the
Eiffel Tower.

contributed immeasurably to the visual style and technical innovation of *Funny Face*, which has come increasingly to be admired and appreciated over the years.

Donen, his cast, and the crew flew to Paris for location filming. Audrey and Mel took a suite at the Hôtel Raphaël, the first of such transitory addresses to become the scene of an eccentric, endearing and exhausting 'domestic' routine, conjured by Audrey to take care of her need to feel rooted and secure. She had not yet acquired a home of her own (the Burgenstock chalet and the London apartment were rented), but she and Mel had collected numerous portable possessions, among them beautiful linen, pictures, a pair of silver candlesticks, ashtrays, crockery, cutlery, books, a record-player and records.

Briefing the new
'Quality' woman.

On checking into the Raphaël, she requested the removal of the hotel's own linen and ornaments, rearranged the furniture, and unpacked several trunks of her treasures. She reasoned that by bringing her personal touch to the anonymity of hotel rooms, however grandly appointed, she could create the comforting illusion of a home, taking evening meals with her husband in an environment made cosy and individual. In years to come, it would be rumoured that she travelled, at vast expense, with up to fifty-five pieces of luggage. Audrey needed the security of money in the bank, but she spent whatever was required to satisfy her quest for stability, and her need for comfort rather than luxury.

Paris, that most beautiful of cities with its wide boulevards, the chestnut trees in bloom, its

In *Funny Face* the world of fashion photography invades the Greenwich Village bookshop where earnest blue-stocking Jo Stockton (Hepburn, on ladder) works.

gracious buildings and chic citizens, its special sense of life lived to the full, and the innate grace and style that permeates the place, was a natural habitat for Audrey. She blossomed in the atmosphere of what was, for once, a happy shoot, in a city to whose culture she responded. Then, too, she had Mel, her emotional prop, on hand but busy with his own film, which left Audrey with a certain independence. Her shy personality seemed to grow more

open and expansive, her sense of fun was evident, and she displayed a new air of maturity.

On screen, however, she makes her first appearance, atop a ladder in the bookshop, looking a good decade younger than her twenty-seven years. At once tremulous and defiant as she tries to evict Maggie (Kay Thompson) and her troupe of models from the store, she melts into wonderment when Astaire kisses her. He exits, leaving her in her little smock

amidst a pile of books to sing 'How Long Has This Been Going On?'

When Dick is persuading Maggie to use Jo as her new model, he says, 'She's new, she's fresh . . .' Maggie replies, 'I think her face is perfectly funny — the "Quality" woman must have grace, elegance, and bezazz.' Dick counters, 'All our girls have grace, elegance and bezazz. What's wrong with bringing out a girl who has character, spirit and intelligence?'

During the course of the film, Audrey/Jo amply displays all six of the qualities to which Dick refers. The lines might have been directly written about Audrey. Even more so, the sentiments she expressed about herself in life are echoed in the scene in which Dick encourages her to accept the assignment. She says, wide-eyed with disbelief, 'How could I be a model? I've no illusions about my looks — I think my face is funny.' Dick responds, 'What you call funny, I call interesting.'

In Paris, Givenchy transforms this Cinderella character into a fashion plate of breathtaking elegance and beauty, without forfeiting her uncorrupted freshness. The film unveils a series of stunning clothes in black, in white and in glorious combinations of pastel colours, photographed in

awaiting their guru. It is here that Audrey immortalised the uniform of black polo-neck sweater and matching tight pants, excelling in a dance routine that ribs the earnest modern dance of the 1950s intellectual avant-garde. Dilys Powell felt that the jokes 'visually sometimes go off with a bang – as when Miss Hepburn, looking in her black tight pants and pullover like an amiable miniature version of Conrad Veidt in *Caligari*, brilliantly executes an Empathicalist's dance.'

The only real problem the company had to face was the unseasonal and incessant rain, which bedevilled Donen and caused him to run over schedule. It made Fred and Audrey's romantic *pas de deux* in Chantilly, where they dance on grass, a difficult and muddy grind. Audrey remarked, 'Here I've been waiting twenty years to dance with Fred Astaire, and what do I get? Mud!' But the wet weather also proved serendipitous to the shooting of the balloon sequence: Donen was forced to film in a downpour, umbrellas were brought into the scene and it achieved an originality beyond the intended image in spring sunshine.

Funny Face is a summation of Audrey Hepburn's magic essence, and signifies much that is important in her career. It was the

only full-blooded 'Hollywood' musical she made, in which she really got to dance and sing, and it is a performance to cherish. The movie made manifest the fruits of her association with Givenchy – indeed, in terms of the sheer *range* of the clothes, one might see it as the apogee of his on-screen designs for her. The Parisian setting, the gloss and the sheer infectious fun of the film also set something of a

'He Loves and She Loves' – the 'Wedding Dance'. Coping with muddy grass at Chantilly.

Opposite: Doing an Empathicalist's dance in a smoky Left Bank cellar, and immortalising the black polo-neck sweater in the process.

trend for Audrey. It proved to be the first of five films she would make in Paris, and although they vary enormously in content, they have a connecting link in tone and in the actress's style, which marks them out from the other material she tackled.

As a piece of sheer film-musical artistry, *Funny Face* remains collectable for lovers of the genre, with Fred Astaire providing dazzling dance solos. On a more negative note, it gave rise to the first rumblings of criticism in relation to Audrey's aged leading men. She and Astaire got away with it, thanks to his spry grace and good-natured, unthreatening charm, but her next outing would

provoke a measure of complaint.

Astaire recalled, 'The picture was such a complete joy that we all hated to see it end.' Audrey may well have shared the sentiments, but she was once again very tired and in need of a rest. As it turned out, she had only four weeks in which to relax: a quick shopping trip to London, a vacation with Mel in the Burgenstock chalet, and she was back in her suite at the Raphaël to begin work on her fifth American picture – her fourth as a star, and her second and last with Billy Wilder.

While the filming of *Funny Face* was in progress, Wilder had got to work on Claude Anet's

Ariane, a novel about a young female cellist in love with a much older man, which had been filmed in Berlin with Elisabeth Bergner in 1931. Wilder made several changes to the original. He re-set the story in Paris, made Ariane the daughter of a widowed private detective, and conceived the object of her affections as a Howard Hughes-style billionaire and a scandalously unrepentant *roué*. On the search for a new writing collaborator, he found I.A.L. Diamond, a Romanian immigrant and a genius of comedy writing. He set Diamond to work, beginning a brilliant partnership that was later to result in *Some Like It Hot* and *The Apartment*.

Retitled *Love in the Afternoon*, the film tells how Ariane Chavasse, a seventeen-year-old cello-playing music student, becomes fascinated by Frank Flannagan, the subject of one of her father's investigations. Overhearing Chavasse's client, an outraged husband, telling her father that he is off to the Ritz to shoot Flannagan, she worms her way into the latter's suite to warn him. Fascinated by this mysterious girl who refuses even to divulge her name, he invites her to visit him the next afternoon. There follows a series of trysts, during which she falls in love with him while pretending to be a

In Billy Wilder's *Love in the Afternoon*, widowed detective Chavasse (Maurice Chevalier) is concerned about his daughter Ariane's odd behaviour.

Afternoon romance *al fresco*.

sophisticated woman with a string of jet-set lovers.

It is a charming and romantic story, perfect for Hepburn's particular brand of romantic wonderment and throw-away wit. Maurice Chevalier, giving perhaps the best screen-acting performance of his career, is superb as Ariane's father. Much of the action takes place at the Ritz, brilliantly reconstructed at the Boulogne studios by Alexander Trauner, and there is a running musical gag worthy – as are many delightful touches in the film – of Wilder's

Gary Cooper, his age disguised by deliberately low-key lighting, is playboy Frank Flannagan, intrigued by this mysterious young woman.

mentor, Ernst Lubitsch. Viewed now (difficult, since it is rarely shown), *Love in the Afternoon*, which immortalised the tune 'Fascination', is rich in European grace and wit, as well as intriguing moral ambiguity. It was not a success. As with *Sabrina*, Billy Wilder saw the film as an ideal vehicle for Cary Grant, ageing but still devastatingly attractive, and with a gift for romantic comedy that has seldom been equalled, let alone surpassed. Alas, once again, Grant proved unavailable, and the director hit upon Gary Cooper to play Frank Flannagan.

Tall, lean and macho, Cooper had been a much-loved star since 1926. He successfully bridged the change from silents to sound, twice winning an Oscar and remaining every woman's ideal of the strong, silent type throughout his career. As notorious a

womaniser as the character Wilder called upon him to play, he had a shy, monosyllabic charm, and was renowned for his superbly tailored clothes. He had ventured into comedy, but it was not his strongest suit, while as a dancer he had two left feet, which bedevilled a key scene in the film. At fifty-six, Cooper looked drawn and much older than his years. He suffered from recurrent hernias and a duodenal ulcer, precursors of the cancer that was to kill him four and a half years later.

It was soon clear that the May-December romance of Frank and Ariane was in danger of suffering from Cooper's gaunt and ageing features. Wilder took care of the problem by filming him through gauze filters, upstaging him, and keeping him in the shadows of the stylish black-and-white photography – and that is what is wrong with the finished product.

Flannagan, in at least two-thirds of his scenes, is muffled as a character and a personality and, if anything, the attempt to take the curse off his age draws attention to it.

For all that, the film has much to offer, and it was another trouble-free engagement for Audrey. She and Cooper got along extremely well – and he managed to keep a safe distance from her off the screen. Mel was in the South of France filming *The Vintage*, but she would fly to Nice at weekends, which they spent at St Tropez. It was at this time that Mel gave Audrey a little Yorkshire terrier, which she christened Famous and on which she lavished all the adoration, care, attention and red ribbons that she was longing to give to a child.

When *Love in the Afternoon* was released the following year, the so-called upholders of public decency stayed away in their droves from what they considered an immoral film. *Variety* called the casting of Cooper 'curious', although he found favour with the *New York Times*. Again, as in *Funny Face*, the screenplay gave Audrey dialogue that she might have written about herself. In a tender scene with Cooper, she says, 'I'm too thin and my ears stick out and my teeth are crooked and my neck's *much* too long.' To which

he rejoins, 'Maybe so, but I love the way it all hangs together.'

So did the critics, but for all the plaudits she – and in some quarters, Cooper and the film – garnered, discomfort about the age difference of the stars remained strong and the film died at the box office.

War and Peace had been released in August and had met with a lukewarm critical reception. Once again, there were valentines for Audrey, but delivered with slightly less enthusiasm than usual. None the less, she remained in favour, and offers of work did not diminish. Twentieth Century-Fox wanted her to star in Françoise Sagan's *A Certain Smile* and to play Anne Frank; she was invited to take over from Diane Cilento in the stage musical *Zuleika*; Associated British Pictures were still trying to find a vehicle for her.

Audrey said no to all of them. She was tired and fretful. She had worked too hard for too long – and she wanted a child. The only commitment she made was to NBC, honouring a promise to appear in *Mayerling*, a ninety-minute TV film special, opposite her husband. This was to be made in New York in January, which allowed the Ferrers to take a much-needed break in the sun near Palm Springs.

The picture tells the story: Mel and Audrey were a joint disaster in *Mayerling*, an expensive failure for NBC TV and the last time they acted together.

The budget for *Mayerling* was astronomical, the sets and costumes were opulent, the supporting actors were Diana Wynyard and Raymond Massey, the director Anatole Litvak. But for all the resources lavished upon it, this tale of the passionate love affair between Crown Prince Rudolf of Austria and his mistress, Marie Vetsera, culminating in a double suicide, was an absolute failure. Mel and Audrey may have worshipped each other in life, but

on the screen they failed to ignite the necessary spark. Mel was essentially miscast — too old, too cold — and the general opinion of the enterprise was summed up by critic John Crosby, who commented, 'The lovers seem more fated to bore each other to death than to end their illicit alliance in a murder-suicide pact.'

With no plans announced for her next movie, the indifferent response to *War and Peace* and the failure of *Mayerling*, people

might have been forgiven for thinking the Hepburn roll was over. In February 1957, however, while she and Mel were still in New York, she finally stopped resisting a challenging offer which had been made by Warner Brothers but which would involve a long separation from her husband. What she couldn't know at that time was that she would be embarking on the most substantial film of her entire career.

ACTS OF FAITH

As Sister Luke in *The Nun's Story*, assisting Dr Fortunati (Peter Finch).

What has always helped me a great deal are the clothes . . .
Once you're in that habit, of a nun, it's not that you become
a saint, but you walk differently, you feel something

AUDREY HEPBURN

Audrey made one believe that she really, really wanted to
be a nun, and had a terrible time breaking off and leaving.
It's all there, and I know very few other people who could
have done it – I'm not sure I know anybody

FRED ZINNEMANN

Like several of his colleagues, including Billy Wilder, Fred Zinnemann was a Viennese-born Jew of the old school – disciplined, educated and cultivated. He trained in Paris, becoming an assistant cameraman, before leaving for the USA in 1929. In Hollywood, he served a long apprenticeship in various capacities, but first made his mark as a documentary film-maker with *The Wave* in 1934. In 1937 Zinnemann was signed to direct short films for MGM, one of which – *That Mothers Might Live* – won him an Oscar.

His first feature was *The Search* (1948), the heart-rending tale of an American soldier and a dispossessed child searching for the boy's mother amid the ruins and displaced persons' camps of post-war Germany. Zinnemann cast an actor unknown to cinema audiences, Montgomery Clift, as the soldier, displaying a rare instinct for casting which was to afford Marlon Brando his first film role in Zinnemann's *The Men* (1949).

By 1957 the director had climbed to the top of his profession. A fine photographer himself, he displayed a mastery of visual composition, catholicity of subject matter, and innate good taste. His major successes had included the Oscar-nominated

High Noon (1952), which introduced Grace Kelly, and *From Here to Eternity* (1953), which famously cast Deborah Kerr against type as the unhappy, faithless army wife who succumbs to Burt Lancaster on a beach. As well as bringing Frank Sinatra an acting Oscar, *From Here to Eternity* won the Academy Awards for Best Picture and Best Director, as would *A Man for All Seasons* in 1966.

Doubtless, Zinnemann was one of the directors to whom Audrey was referring when, in a television interview with Professor Richard Brown in 1990, she said, 'I was so terribly lucky to – really, by chance – fall into movie-making at a period when these directors were around and wanted me, and that has been the sort of *miracle* of my career . . . I wasn't a tearing beauty; I didn't have any way for them to know whether I could really act. I was in the hands of these people.'

Audrey had met Zinnemann in 1954, when Mike Todd was hoping to produce *War and Peace* with Zinnemann as director. In the midst of the uncertainty surrounding the project, Fred and his wife Renée dined with Audrey and Mel in a Lucerne restaurant. Director and actress got along extremely well, and there was 'a mutual sense' of wanting to work

together. They parted determined to do so.

With *War and Peace* lost to De Laurentiis and Vidor, another opportunity came along two years later. Gary Cooper read a novel by Kathryn Hulme called *The Nun's Story*, and, thinking it might appeal to Fred, sent it to him. Cooper was right. Zinnemann started the rounds of attempting to interest a studio in the material, but met with a negative response everywhere. The general attitude was summed up in the comment 'Who wants to see a documentary about how to become a nun?'

This opinion was dramatically reversed when Audrey Hepburn became a candidate for the central role, and a deal was concluded with Warner Brothers. But despite her enthusiasm for the story, Audrey hesitated to commit herself. A major stumbling block was that filming would take her to the Belgian Congo (now Zaïre), not only threatening her fragile health in the humidity and relatively rough conditions of the African tropics, but separating her from Mel for some considerable time. And she wanted to have a baby. It was Mel, together with her agent, Kurt Frings, who persuaded her to accept the offer.

In the spring of 1957, however, *The Nun's Story* was a long way off from shooting. It was a massive project, which involved Zinnemann in eighteen months of work, beginning with getting a screenplay written, and undertaking the delicate and protracted task of seeking co-operation from the Catholic Church authorities.

While writer Robert Anderson worked on the script, and Zinnemann immersed himself in the complex pre-production tasks, Audrey was free. After a fortnight's skiing in Switzerland, she went to Madrid with Mel, who had a part in *The Sun Also Rises*. The cast was headed by Tyrone Power, Ava Gardner and Errol Flynn; the French 'existentialist' singer Juliette Gréco was also in it, and the writer of the screenplay, Peter Viertel – son of Fred Zinnemann's mentor, Berthold Viertel, and future husband of Deborah Kerr – was also present. It made for an interesting and enjoyable time. Audrey and Mel often dined with Power and Ava Gardner, while Ava and Audrey became good friends, going on shopping expeditions at the weekends, with a beribboned Famous in tow.

When locations switched to Mexico City, Audrey accompanied Mel. She almost never visited the set and spent a quiet time in the Mexican sun. From there the couple flew to the States, visiting Mel's family in Santa Barbara and on Long Island. Back in Burgenstock, Audrey read Anderson's completed screenplay, and learned that New York society columnist Cholly Knickerbocker had named her one of the ten 'Most Fascinating Women in the World'. Her old friend the British photographer Anthony Beauchamp had similarly eulogised her in his 'Ten Loveliest Women' list, while the New York Dress Institute had voted her the sixth-best-dressed woman in the world. *Funny Face* and *Love in the Afternoon* had both been released, the first to a generally enthusiastic reception.

Audrey was able to enjoy what was, for her, a reasonably lengthy respite living a normal life. It was during this time that Mel conceived the idea of filming *Green Mansions*, with himself directing his wife in the lead role of Rima the Bird Girl. W.H. Hudson's novel, written early in the twentieth century and set in the jungles of Venezuela in the late nineteenth, was once a popular adventure romance. While traversing the South American jungle, Abel, an explorer, encounters Rima, a strange, elusive and other-worldly creature, able to talk to birds and other animals. He is drawn to Rima – whose 'figure and features were

singularly delicate' – as if by a magnet, but is unable to hold on to her. One can detect a faint echo of Ondine in Rima and her relationship with the explorer, but this time it is she who meets her death, burnt at the stake by an Indian tribe who interpret her humane perfection as emanating from an evil spirit.

Audrey, too, loved the book and the couple flew to LA to try to secure a deal. There they learned that they were not the first people to be attracted to it. RKO had bought the property as a vehicle for Dolores Del Rio but never made the picture. Eleven years later, an independent producer bought it for a nominal sum and immediately sold it at a profit to MGM. Over a period of eight years, various writers at Metro were assigned to adapt it, but none of the results met with Louis B. Mayer's approval. In 1953, Alan Jay Lerner had a go at the material, and it was finally given a green light with Vincente Minnelli to direct on location in South America, and Pier Angeli as Rima. Much pre-production progress had been made when, once again, the project was dropped as a result of new management policies at the studio.

Generally, a property with this kind of history would stand little or no chance of getting off the ground, but producer Edmund Grainger was willing to take it on, and with the strength of Audrey Hepburn's name, persuaded MGM – who still had grave doubts about the story's commercial viability – to resuscitate the project. Dorothy Kingsley was hired to write the screenplay, and the Ferrers spent much of the spring in Hollywood – Mel in discussions with Kingsley and MGM, Audrey conferring with Zinnemann, Robert Anderson, and the producer on *The Nun's Story*, Henry Blanke.

During this period, Audrey met both Kathryn Hulme and Marie-Louise Habets, on whose true story Miss Hulme had based her novel. The two women had met at a United Nations refugee camp in Germany after the war, where Kathryn was in command and Marie-Louise was nursing. They became friends and Marie-Louise was finally persuaded to tell the story of how she, a devout Catholic nun and dedicated missionary nurse, broke her vows in order to work with the Belgian Resistance movement against the Nazis. The story of her seventeen years in the convent and the Congo, and the agony of her subsequent leave-taking, formed the substance of *The Nun's Story*, its main character now called Gabrielle Van Der Mal.

The Nun's Story opens with the young Gabrielle Van Der Mal preparing to leave her family to enter a convent. Gabrielle is the loving daughter of a famous surgeon. Her burning goal is to become a medical missionary nun in the Congo, and she joins an order specialising in sending their sisters there.

During her term as, first, a postulant, then a novice, Gabrielle, now Sister Luke, struggles to come to terms with her vows of obedience, finding it agonisingly difficult to bury her natural streak of independence, or the intense pride she takes in her work. Her superiors, realising that she is not yet at one with what they call 'the religious life', place every kind of disciplinary obstacle in her way before finally despatching her to the Congo where she assists Dr Fortunati, the dishevelled, outspoken and inspirationally brilliant medical man who runs the Congo hospital. She impresses him with her exceptional skills and her individuality; in turn, he adds to the inner struggles of her conscience by voicing his own doubts about her suitability for convent life.

After a bout of TB, from which she recovers, Sister Luke – who has won an exceptional degree of love and devotion from the native

people, and from her fellow sisters – is sent back to Belgium as escort to a seriously ill patient. She finds the resumption of life in the cloisters almost intolerable, but all thoughts of a return to Africa are halted by the outbreak of war. Finally sent as a surgical assistant to a hospital on the Holland-Belgium border, she finds herself behaving contrary to her orders by aiding a Resistance worker. When she receives word that her beloved father has been killed in a Nazi ambush, unchristian feelings of hatred against the enemy assail her. After seventeen years of struggle, she decides to go out into the world to work for the underground movement.

It is easy to see why Audrey was drawn to the story, and particularly responsive to its close associations with her own past. She formed a strong bond with Marie-Louise Habets, who worked privately with her on the conduct of a nun's life and taught her many things, including correct handling of surgical instruments for the hospital scenes.

During the summer, Audrey went with Mel to Germany where he was making a film called *Fräulein*. By the autumn, serious preparations were under way for *The Nun's Story*. A heavyweight cast included two superlative actresses of the British theatre,

Dame Edith Evans and Peggy (later Dame Peggy) Ashcroft, playing Sister Luke's Mother Superiors in Belgium and the Congo respectively. The key role of Dr Fortunati went to the Australian actor Peter Finch. This time, there was to be no romance for Audrey's character, only a subtly implied attraction between the doctor and Sister Luke. Finch was a well-known hell-raiser, drinker and womaniser; he was also a fine actor, and proved an astute choice, very much in command of his own scenes and a perfect foil to Audrey.

Location work was scheduled for Belgium, but the Sisters of Charity convent and the Bishop of Bruges refused permission to film on the actual premises. The accomplished Alexander Trauner, entrusted with the production design, reconstructed the convent and chapel, right down to the statuary, at Rome's Cinecittà studios. It is almost impossible to identify them as sets, so realistically were they built. For the long segment in the Congo, the unit was to be based in Stanleyville, travelling up-river from there to an actual leper colony which Sister Luke must visit in the course of her duties. To Audrey's delight, Franz Planer was to photograph the film and, once again, her request was granted for Alberto and Grazia de Rossi to take care of her make-up and hair.

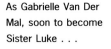

As Gabrielle Van Der Mal, soon to become Sister Luke . . .

. . . at the solemn
vows ceremony.

Audrey wished to spend a few days in a convent absorbing the authentic atmosphere and observing the actual deportment of the nuns. The Belgian orders were adamant in their refusal, but a French order was more co-operative. In the event, all of Zinnemann's main 'nuns' took this route to prepare for their roles, each being despatched to a different French convent. The dedication shows in the finished product, and Audrey herself benefits from being surrounded by actresses of high quality in substantial roles.

Scheduling *Green Mansions* had proved something of a problem.

Eventually, it was decided that Mel would use the period of Audrey's absence to visit Venezuela and other South American countries to shoot the exterior backgrounds for his film. Audrey was nervy about the long time and the distance that was soon to be between them, and distressed at her failure to fall pregnant again. She lavished her frustrated mother-love on Famous, and was distraught to learn that quarantine laws would not allow him into the Congo. Such was her distress that every kind of influence was brought to bear on the authorities and finally, after the dog had received all the

Rehearsing with director Fred Zinnemann in the leper colony in the Congo.

necessary inoculations, the rules were bent.

Audrey (and Famous) arrived in Rome at the beginning of January 1958 for preliminary work. She checked in to the Hassler Hotel, unhappy that the film had not yet had a finishing date confirmed, and under some pressure because, having insisted on spending Christmas with Mel, she had only nine days in which to complete the preparations before departing for the Congo.

On 16 January 1958, Zinnemann and his company took the fourteen-hour flight to Stanleyville. They settled in simple but comfortable lodgings at the Sabena Guest House, where

provisions arrived twice a week from Belgium to feed them. In their three months there, they fell in love with the place and its people, little realising that a bloody revolution was only a year away – a revolution that would leave many of the people they knew, and some of the Congo's real nuns, dead.

In his autobiography, Fred Zinnemann writes, 'I have never seen anyone more disciplined, more gracious or more dedicated to her work than Audrey. There was no ego, no asking for favours; there was the greatest consideration for her co-workers. The only thing she requested in the Congo, where the temperature hovered around ninety-five degrees and the humidity was incredible, was an air-conditioner. It was promptly sent from the studio in Burbank but did not seem to do much good. On closer inspection it turned out to be a humidifier!'

Contrary to the generally-held view of Audrey's frailty, Zinnemann said she 'looked very delicate, but actually she was very tough physically. She was in practically every shot that we made in the entire film. She had to take a day and a half off because she had a kidney stone – you can imagine, a day and a half in the Congo. It was extraordinary.'

When the unit returned to Rome for interior shooting, Audrey was taken ill again, this time rather more seriously. The Baroness, who had visited her regularly in Paris during her previous filming there, came to look after her. A visit from brother Ian – now a businessman in The Hague – and his wife and young child brought cheer, and also the quaint suggestion from Audrey that he should pose for the photograph of Gabrielle's fiancé which is briefly seen in the film. This he did. The recurrence of her kidney problem confined Audrey to bed for several days, leaving her miserable at the thought that she was causing

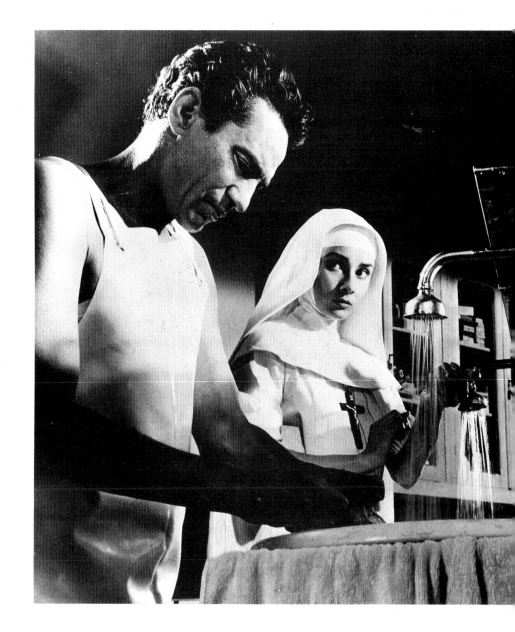

With Dr Fortunati in the laboratory where she diagnoses her own tuberculosis.

problems for Zinnemann and her colleagues, and adding to worries about the forthcoming *Green Mansions*, repeatedly delayed on her account.

Mel visited her during her illness and told her that *Green Mansions* would be made at MGM studios, using exterior footage that he had brought back from his South

At the convent in
Belgium, acquiring
obedience and humility
through the
performance of menial
tasks.

The novice.

American travels. The problems of time and expense were so great as to prevent location filming as he had originally intended; and there was the further consideration that Audrey could not have been expected to withstand the jungles of Venezuela and Colombia after her long and exhausting stint in the Congo.

The Nun's Story is a majestic film. It moves from its early sequences in the imposing confines of the convent, through the harrowing scenes in a madhouse run by the nuns where Sister Luke is sent to work, and the Congo episodes, rich in a sense of life and missionary selflessness, to the stultifying agony of Sister Luke's return to the convent, her inner struggle, and her silent, lonely and courageous exit to the outside world. Dignified and moving, it is directed with a sure hand and a keen eye for detail, the excellence of director and cast being matched in every department.

Considered by many to be the best English-language film ever made on the subject of the monastic life, it is without doubt the weightiest film in which Audrey Hepburn appeared. She brings a deeply-felt and moving sincerity to the role. Her natural vulnerability is counterpointed by elements of steely strength and moments of touching serenity.

Although she is the central character, she, and Fred Zinnemann, subsume their work in the common cause of authenticity; in all the group scenes in the convent, she is one of a crowd. But the individual touches in her performance are subtle and telling – a performance of nuance in a film of nuance and sober weight.

Fred Zinnemann said of her, 'Looking at the film again, after more than twenty-five years, I am struck by the fine, firm line of development in Audrey's performance. The subconscious quality of independence is present in all her actions. When she comes running in late for the Service, her haste betrays the inner calm she should be developing; or the time when the girls are admitted as postulants and prostrate themselves on the floor in front of the Mother General, Audrey peeks out of one eye, curiosity getting the better of her. Her performance is put together out of dozens of moments of independence . . .' Audrey had, as Fred Zinnemann says, 'real humility' and it shows in the film to her advantage.

She finished work in June after completing locations in Belgium, where she had visited her birthplace before flying to Hollywood to begin work on her husband's picture. The tall, dark and handsome Anthony Perkins

Quiet reflection
between takes.

was to play Abel. His sensitive, haunted features were almost as striking as Audrey's. A rising star, only three years older than his co-star, he was her first young leading man – although, ironically, in this case the screenplay had rewritten the character, who in the book is much older. Also in the cast, playing an Indian, was the famous Japanese-American silent-screen actor Sessue Hayakawa.

A large swathe of the MGM backlot had been given over to the construction of the *Green Mansions* sets. Many acres of open lot were converted into a realistic river area, and art director Preston Ames was able to use materials and plants that Mel had had shipped in from South America, together with tropical birds. The background footage Mel had shot, combined with the impressive settings which included a complete Indian village, made for a very convincing environment.

In the film, Rima has a young fawn as her constant companion. Fawns are nervous, sensitive creatures and Mel took advice on how best to deal with this

requirement. The result was that a
baby fawn was brought from a
specialist zoo outside Los Angeles.
According to Charles Higham,
'When the little creature with its
big liquid eyes, supple form, and
skinny legs arrived, everyone
laughed because it looked just like
Audrey' – who was detailed to
rear it like a baby. Despite her
initial qualms about separating it
from its mother, Audrey took the
fawn home to her rented house,
where her love of animals and her
need for motherhood overcame her
resistance.

She lavished care and attention
on Ip, as they named the beautiful
creature, and, as the experts had
predicted, by the time shooting
commenced, Ip thought Audrey
was his mother and followed her
about as required. Rearing Ip,
though, was not an altogether
easy task – rather like a goat, he
had a tendency to eat anything
and everything in sight, and on
one occasion he managed to get
out. Although he was found,
sleeping under a tree, this escape
necessitated keeping all the
downstairs windows closed from
then on. Famous, apparently, was
not too troubled by his new
temporary companion.

More difficult was the question
of the photographic process to be
used for the film. This was the era
of CinemaScope; but when

cinematographer Joseph
Ruttenberg's test footage was
developed, the width of Audrey's
face was so pronounced as to
render the CinemaScope lens
unusable. She had always asserted

that her face was too wide, but
was horrified at what she saw. The
problem was finally solved by
Robert Gottschalk, the creator of
Panavision – the process that
would soon supersede CinemaScope

lp the fawn learns to
live with and love
Audrey . . .

. . . and Famous!

– who worked on a new lens to rectify the image.

Early in the rehearsal period, Audrey was severely shaken and upset by an accident that occurred when she was driving her rented car in Beverly Hills. Forced off the road by a reckless oncoming vehicle, she collided with a parked car. What turned this relatively minor crash into a traumatic event was a young aspiring actress-dancer named Joan Lora, who was sitting in the stationary vehicle at the time. Miss Lora maintained that she suffered serious back injuries from the force of the collision and that her career prospects were ruined. She sued Audrey for $45,000 compensation in a protracted action. The ruling, long after the event, in fact cost Audrey $4,500, the court having concluded that Audrey hadn't been travelling anywhere near fast enough to cause the amount of damage that Miss Lora had claimed. But it wasn't the money that caused Audrey severe distress – it was the thought that she was responsible for somebody else's suffering. She refused to drive again for some time.

However, filming proceeded smoothly enough and, by all accounts, being directed by her husband, particularly in the love scenes, seemed to suit Audrey.

Mel, for once truly in the driving seat, was pleased with the results of his efforts. It must have been a bitter blow, therefore, when *Green Mansions* was released in the spring of 1959 to a largely negative reception.

There are those who like this film but, in general, its greenish-colour hue did not find favour, and its elusive plot was considered far too 'literary' to work on the screen. *Variety* thought it 'likely to confuse those who haven't read the book and irritate those who have'. On this occasion, the show-biz 'bible' didn't have compliments even for Audrey, although they commented favourably on her looks.

Audrey's most ardent fan among the critics, Bosley Crowther of the *New York Times*, wrote that the producer's achievement was to get 'the slender and soulful Audrey Hepburn to play Rima . . . without the ethereal Miss Hepburn vaporing lightly through the Venezuelan woods, this could be a pretty foolish film.' Crowther also felt that the actress displayed 'grace and dignity, making Rima both poignant and idyllic, if not in the least logical'. The film was an out-and-out failure at the box office, and has rarely been seen since.

Some weeks later, *The Nun's Story* opened to rapturous reviews,

huge crowds at the box office and six Academy Award nominations, including Best Picture, Best Director and Best Actress. This was wonderful news for Audrey, conclusively burying the memory of *Green Mansions* in the public mind, but it must have poured salt in Mel's wounds.

Sadly for Fred Zinnemann and Audrey, they were up against another 'religious' film, William Wyler's epic remake of *Ben-Hur*, and it was this film that swept the board at the Oscar ceremony – except for Best Actress, which went not to Audrey, but to French actress Simone Signoret for her performance in the British film *Room at the Top*. In looking back on Audrey's career, it is a matter for regret that she failed to capture the highest industry accolade for Sister Luke. The *New York Times* recognised this was 'a soaring and luminous film' in which Audrey Hepburn 'has her most demanding film role and gives her finest performance'. She received the New York Critics' Award for Best Actress and the British Academy Award.

By the time all this happened, however, Audrey was hard at work on a new and challenging picture. More significantly, she began filming in the knowledge that she was once again pregnant.

A New Life

Breakfast at Tiffany's: wake-up time for Holly and 'Cat'.

8

Like all new mothers, I couldn't believe at first he was really for me and that I could keep him

AUDREY HEPBURN

'Moon River' was written for her. No one else has ever understood it so completely. There have been more than a thousand versions of 'Moon River', but hers is unquestionably the greatest

HENRY MANCINI

John Huston, the son of actor Walter and father of actress-to-be Anjelica, was in every regard a larger-than-life character. A maverick writer-director with a picaresque past, this huge man of flamboyant personality had, in the course of his youth, been an amateur boxer and a cavalry officer in the Mexican army. He had studied painting in Paris, making a living by sketching tourists, and slept rough in London, feeding himself by singing on street corners. He had played a few small parts for William Wyler in Hollywood, written short stories, and briefly been a news reporter in New York.

In the late 1930s, Huston, who had had a previous stint in the writers' department at Goldwyn studios, buckled down to screenwriting, through which he began a long and rich association with Humphrey Bogart. He hit the jackpot with his first directorial assignment, *The Maltese Falcon* (1941), and by 1959 his major successes included *The Treasure of the Sierra Madre*, *The Asphalt Jungle*, and *The African Queen* (with Bogart and 'the other Hepburn'). Prolific, erratic and contradictory, Huston was a macho, hard-drinking womaniser, who lived the life of a landed gentleman in Ireland between jobs, and devoted much of his time, energy and money to fostering his substantial art collection. He was capable of great consideration and kindness to actors, and equally capable of cruelty and destructiveness. The most famous example of the latter was to be his treatment of Montgomery Clift on *Freud*.

In 1958, screenwriter Ben Maddow approached Huston with his screenplay of *The Unforgiven*, a revenge Western to be produced by Hecht-Hill-Lancaster with a cast headed by Burt Lancaster and Audrey Hepburn. In his autobiography Huston recalled, 'I thought I saw in Maddow's script the potential for a more serious — and better — film than either he or Hecht-Hill-Lancaster had originally contemplated. I wanted to turn it into the story of racial intolerance in a frontier town, a comment on the real nature of community "morality". The trouble was that the producers disagreed . . .

'This difference of intention did not become an issue until we were very close to shooting time, and quite mistakenly I agreed to stick it out, thus violating my own conviction that a picture-maker should undertake nothing but what he believes in.'

There is little reason to doubt these sentiments, but according to Huston's biographer, Lawrence Grobel, he had other motives for continuing with the project. Apart from the lure of a substantial paycheck, there was the prospect of filming on location in Mexico. Huston was in partnership with a man called Billy Pearson, who was masterminding the acquisition of pre-Columbian Mexican treasures – illegally. The film would provide the director with a golden opportunity to be in close touch with this venture.

In retrospect, Audrey's decision to accept the role of Rachel Zachary was misguided. She was hardly ideal casting, and had to face working in tough conditions during her pregnancy. Durango and its surrounding environs were chosen for the location because of the still-unspoilt landscape. Indeed, it was harsh and primitive. The dry earth was baked hard and cracked by the heat; strong winds blew dust and sand everywhere, caking the cast and crew with grime; living conditions in the local hotel were basic. One comfort was the presence of Audrey's beloved Franz Planer as lighting cameraman. Then, too, she was very nervous about having to ride, but acquiesced in the interests of the film. She took lessons, and was given a horse, named Diabolo, which had belonged to President Batista of Cuba.

Ben Zachary (Burt
Lancaster) restrains
Rachel from returning
to her people in *The
Unforgiven*.

The plot of *The Unforgiven*
focuses on the Zacharys – widowed
mother, three sons and a daughter
– a family of hardened frontier
ranchers. Rachel is a Kiowa
Indian, stolen from her tribe in
babyhood by the the late Will
Zachary and adopted by him and
his wife (Lillian Gish). She and her
brothers believe she was the
foundling baby of massacred white
pioneers. The secret of her birth
remains intact until a vengeful
former crony of old man Zachary's
reveals the truth.

Rachel and her eldest brother
Ben (Burt Lancaster) are devoted
to each other. Their feelings are
not entirely familial and, by the
end of the film, after defending
themselves against marauding
Kiowas, including Rachel's blood
brother whom she is forced to

shoot in self-defence, they are to
marry. The role, which presented
Audrey with a new challenge of
characterisation, must have
seemed a good opportunity to get
away from her more usual image.
It was also a chance to work with
superstar Lancaster and the
revered veteran Gish, as well as
with a director who was a very
different animal from the
venerable gentlemen who had
guided her career so far.

In the event, there were many
tensions on set. A clash of egos
between Huston and Lancaster,
who disliked each other, proved
detrimental to the finished
product. With his mind not wholly
on the task in hand, Huston
under-directed the actors, causing
particular difficulties for Audie
Murphy, America's most decorated
war hero but an insecure and
unstable man, who off the set
very nearly drowned in an
accident while duck-shooting on
the Durango lake. The director
was also caught in numerous off-
set entanglements with mistresses
past and present who were part of
the production team.

He was, however, kind and
gentle with Audrey, and with
Lillian Gish, while not giving
them much assistance. Gish felt
that he didn't do justice to
Audrey – 'Audrey had great
talent, and he never used it.'

When it came to shooting Audrey's key riding scenes with Diabolo, disaster struck. Thrown from the horse, she landed on her back and had to be rushed to the hospital in Durango, in intense pain. Her major concern was for Mel, from whom she wanted to keep the news. He arrived the next day from Los Angeles, enraged at Huston, who he felt should not have asked Audrey to mount a horse in her condition. Huston recalled, 'I felt responsible, having put her on a horse for the first time. No matter that she had had a good teacher, was brought on slowly, and turned out to be a natural rider. When her horse bolted and some idiot tried to stop it by throwing up his arms, her fall was on my conscience.'

Audrey's doctor came from California. To her astonishment and delight, he was accompanied by Marie-Louise Habets, 'Sister Luke' of *The Nun's Story*. As soon as Audrey could be moved, she was flown to Los Angeles where she spent three agonising weeks recovering from the fall in which she had broken four vertebrae in her back. She was nursed throughout by Miss Habets, who proved a loyal and devoted friend. Filming was stopped until Audrey could resume work.

The journey back to Durango was unpleasant. Audrey had to wear an uncomfortable neck brace, found the flight difficult, and was unable to sit during the Mexican road journey. As well as being in physical pain, which, characteristically, she endured without complaint, she was desperately anxious about the safety of her expected baby, and dreaded the ordeal of mounting Diabolo again. Matters could not have been helped by Mel's view that she should withdraw from the film, or by his undisguised hostility to John Huston. However, with great courage, Audrey completed the riding scenes without incident.

When *The Unforgiven* was released in 1960, Bosley Crowther thought Audrey 'a bit too polished, too fragile and civilized among such tough and stubborn types as Burt Lancaster'. The film remains a curious addition to her filmography, quite unconnected in flavour to any of her other work. Although sincere, dignified and

On Diabolo, the horse from which she was thrown and badly injured.

moving in the later sequences, she is her usual winsome self in the early ones. She is quite unable to come to grips with a Texan accent, though she clearly worked very hard at *pronouncing* the words accurately; and her almost translucently pink-and-white complexion throughout does not help to convince us that she is a pure-bred Indian.

John Huston's last words on the subject were: 'In the end the worst of it was the picture we made. Some of my pictures I don't care for, but *The Unforgiven* is the only one I actually dislike.'

That may have been 'the worst of it' for Huston. For Audrey, the worst was what she had dreaded — once again, she lost her baby. Distraught and exhausted, she made no more pictures that year, but did participate in a special fashion spread for *Harper's Bazaar*, put together by Richard Avedon. She returned to the Burgenstock where, by the autumn, she discovered that she was pregnant again.

She had been approached by Alfred Hitchcock for a new film he was planning called *No Bail for the Judge*, the story of which he outlined to her. Although she had not yet seen a script, she was keen to work with the master of suspense, and provisional contracts were drawn up. While resting after her miscarriage, she read the screenplay, but when she came to a scene that called for her to be brutally raped, her abhorrence of violence took precedence over her interest. She withdrew from the project, making probably the only enemy she ever had. Hitchcock — vain, arrogant and with little respect for actors, especially women — was outraged. He never forgave her, and the film was never made.

This time, Audrey was taking no risks whatsoever with her pregnancy. She passed the winter and spring in her chalet, resting, reading and taking gentle walks. She even chose separation from Mel, who had to make two films in Rome, rather than risk tiring herself or jeopardising the baby by travelling with him.

On 17 July 1960, after a painful labour, the thirty-year-old Audrey gave birth to a nine-and-a-half-pound baby son. Some weeks later, with his grandmother the Baroness and the American Ambassador to Switzerland in attendance, he was christened Sean Hepburn Ferrer in the little chapel where his parents had been married. The baby's gift from his mother's friend Givenchy was a christening robe; the Ambassador used the occasion to present the infant with an American passport.

In order to keep the

newshounds at bay, Audrey agreed to a press conference at which she said, 'I would like to mix Sean with all kinds of people in all countries, so that he will learn what the world is all about. If he's the right kind of person, he should take his own small part in making the world a better place.' These sentiments reflected her own genuine desire to make the world a 'better place'.

Sean was the centre of Audrey's universe. According to Charles Higham, 'She told friends that this moment was far more important to her than anything in her entire professional career; and indeed her whole life had led up to this moment . . . '

When Sean was three weeks old, Fred and Renée Zinnemann visited the Ferrers and reported them to be blissfully happy; another visitor was Sophia Loren, who lived nearby, and who came often to play with her friend's baby. At the time she, too, was desperately trying to have a child of her own. Audrey's nervous temperament caused her to worry that the baby's presence would make Famous unhappy, but the treasured pet soon settled down with the treasured child. More seriously, in the wake of several European kidnapping incidents, she feared for the safety of her child and worried that the security

measures in the Burgenstock were insufficient. She could hardly bear to let Sean out of her sight, and it was some time before she felt happy about entrusting him to the care of her splendid Italian nanny, Gina.

Offers of work had continued to come in during Audrey's pregnancy, only to be rejected, but one script had aroused her interest: George Axelrod's

adaptation of Truman Capote's fashionable novella *Breakfast at Tiffany's*. As seemed now to be her custom, she was in conflict over whether or not to accept the role. At thirty, she realised she needed to move on from the young innocents in which she had specialised, and recognised that Capote's off-beat heroine, Holly Golightly, would supply a necessary change of image. At the

Audrey and Mel with three-day-old Sean.

same time she was disturbed by the character's amorality and also unconfident of her ability to play the part convincingly – particularly as there was much talk that Capote had wanted it to go to Marilyn Monroe. Then, too, although Audrey loved New York, where the film was to be made, she was unhappy about uprooting Sean, who would have to go with her.

Despite these reported doubts at the time, she told Richard Brown in 1990, '*I* had no misgivings. People around me had misgivings, but I didn't.'

Blake Edwards, who would later marry Julie Andrews, was signed to direct the picture. At the time, although he was a successful screenwriter, Edwards's half-dozen or so directing credits had not yet made the name for him that his later *Pink Panther* films, and those made with his wife, would do. He could have been in no doubt as to the advantages of making a movie with Audrey Hepburn as the star. He flew to Switzerland and, adding his voice to those of Audrey's husband, her mother and her agent, who all felt she should make the picture, Edwards successfully used his powers of persuasion to secure her agreement.

Breakfast at Tiffany's tells the story of Holly Golightly, glamorous and unconventional, who lives in a Manhattan apartment with little furniture, lots of suitcases and a nameless cat. Tiffany's jewellery store is her favourite environment, to be rich is her dream. She scratches a living by accepting fifty dollars for the powder room from a succession of male escorts, whom she refers to as 'rats' and 'super-rats', and receives a regular stipend for carrying messages from

Breakfast at Tiffany's: Paul (George Peppard) comforts a distraught Holly.

Martha confesses that she has realised she does harbour more than friendly feelings for Karen, and commits suicide.

William Wyler made the film version for Goldwyn in 1936, from a screenplay by Miss Hellman retitled *These Three*, and starring Miriam Hopkins as Martha and Merle Oberon as Karen. It was an efficient enough film but a total distortion of the original. Here, the scandal that ruins three lives arises from accusations of heterosexual indiscretions. Now, looking for a new, small-scale project, the director decided to return to the story, this time remaining faithful to the play. Even in 1961 the subject was unwelcome, and there were several problems in attempting to obtain a Production Code seal of approval. This was finally granted, but at the cost of, among other things, never mentioning the word 'lesbian'.

Audrey's misgivings about her image were overcome partly by the fact that it was Wyler who wanted her; partly by the attraction of co-starring with Shirley MacLaine and a splendid supporting cast, with Planer (who had also photographed *Breakfast at Tiffany's*) once again on the camera; and partly, according to Charles Higham, because she 'could also relate to the theme implicit in the script: the necessity

for privacy, the danger of gossip and the love that can transcend sexuality'. Then, too, Audrey was cast as Karen, with James Garner as Joe, and it was Shirley MacLaine who had to find the greater courage and play Martha.

Although she got along immensely well with Shirley MacLaine, whose joky behaviour she enjoyed, and had Sean visit at the studio – where he was petted and cooed over by the entire company – Audrey was tired and, once again, edgy. She, who was never happy in Hollywood, seemed to have difficulty concentrating, and on this occasion was uncharacteristically distracted from the task in hand by her son and her dog. There was a crisis at a vital point in the shooting when Famous escaped into the studio

The Children's Hour: Mrs Tilford (Fay Bainter), Martha Dobie (Shirley MacLaine), Karen Wright (Audrey) and her fiancé Dr Joe Cardin (James Garner) try to wrest the truth from the child Mary (Karen Balkin), whose accusations have shattered all their lives.

streets and Audrey was unable to continue until he was found. Sadly, Famous was killed in Hollywood at the end of that year. He had managed to get out of the Ferrer's rented house, opposite Billy and Audrey Wilder's home on Wilshire Boulevard, and had been caught in a collision between two cars. Audrey was inconsolable.

Little comfort was to be had from the vitriolic reception accorded *The Children's Hour* (*The Loudest Whisper* in Britain), released in March 1962. There is no doubt, as one looks at it again, that it has a coy and dated quality – in retrospect Wyler himself realised that the tone of the piece should have been made more contemporary. However, it is a workmanlike film, in which Fay Bainter's Mrs Tilford (Oscar-nominated in the Best Supporting category), Miriam Hopkins (the original Martha, now playing Martha's aunt), and Karen Balkin as the ghastly child are all first-rate. Shirley MacLaine gives one of the strongest performances of her career as the tragic Martha, and Audrey's portrayal of Karen drew on all her own qualities of sweetness and compassion to produce a luminous and moving characterisation. If the dialogue and approach seem old-fashioned, the emotional impact is none the less there, and it is difficult to understand the degree of venom with which it was greeted.

The critic in *Variety* appreciated the two leads, feeling they 'beautifully complement each other', and thought Audrey's 'soft sensitivity, marvelous projection and emotional understatement result in a memorable portrayal – one of potential Oscar nomination calibre'. And Bosley Crowther, Audrey's most steadfast fan, praised her performance. But the compliments were drowned in the general chorus of disapproval, with Crowther damning the film at some length and saying, among other things, that 'it is hard to believe that Lillian Hellman's famous stage play . . . could have aged into such a cultural antique in the course of three decades . . . but here it is, fidgeting and fuming, like some dotty old doll in bombazine with her mouth sagging open in shocked amazement at the batedly whispered hint that a couple of female schoolteachers could be attached to each other by an "unnatural" love'. *Time* magazine considered the film was assuming that 'the perceptive level of the audience is that of a roomful of producers' relatives', though they had only praise for MacLaine. The *New Yorker*, *Playboy*, and the guru among American film critics, Pauline Kael, were even less complimentary.

It must have been a relief for Audrey to get back to Europe after her long two-picture stint in America and the death of Famous. Mel gave her another Yorkshire terrier that came with the somewhat grand name Assam of Assam. She could take comfort, too, in the fact that at the end of 1961, as well as being awarded a place in the Best Dressed Hall of Fame, she remained one of the five top box-office stars in the world, alongside Elizabeth Taylor, Marilyn Monroe, Doris Day, and her recent co-star Shirley MacLaine.

Above: Sean is the centre of attention for his mother and James Garner in her dressing room.

Left: Being made a .fuss of by two famous stars.

FAIR LADY

With Assam, successor to Famous.

9

If my world were to cave in tomorrow, I'd look back on all the pleasures, excitement and worthwhileness I have been lucky enough to have

AUDREY HEPBURN

To say anything against Audrey Hepburn is like talking against the Church

RADIE HARRIS

An exhausted Audrey returned to the Burgenstock with her husband and son to spend almost a year at home, doing the things she liked best: cooking (especially pasta, which was her favourite food and in the preparation of which she excelled), caring for her child, spending time with her husband, and enjoying the tranquillity and natural beauty of her surroundings.

Audrey, it seemed, had everything she could desire. She had earned respect and devotion from her colleagues in a profession that had brought her fame and wealth; she lived away from the hothouse of Hollywood intrigue and backbiting; she had her beloved son, and a marriage that appeared to be rock-solid. But hairline cracks were starting to show in the fabric of her relationship with Mel. When work separated them, rumours of other women would surface. If, indeed, Mel was straying, his infidelities must have been occasional and discreet, but that was of little comfort to his wife.

Early in 1962, with Mel away filming in Italy, Audrey had a visit from Richard Quine, a well-liked and commercially successful director of pleasant lightweight movies such as the 1955 musical version of *My Sister Eileen*. Quine and George Axelrod were to co-

produce – with Quine directing from Axelrod's screenplay – a romantic comedy for Paramount called *Paris When It Sizzles*. They wanted Audrey for the female lead of Gabrielle Simpson, secretary to a screenwriter. The movie was to be shot in Paris during the summer and seemed an attractive assignment.

During his visit, Quine found Audrey 'sprightly, elfin . . . always delightful, always the epitome of politeness, the perfect hostess'. He joined the ever-growing ranks of those who were completely captivated by her, and was delighted when she accepted the role.

But *Paris When It Sizzles*, far from being a happy return to that city for Audrey, brought trials and tribulations. She was unhappy with the test footage shot by France's renowned Claude Renoir, a superb cinematographer but unversed in the particular requirements of shooting a Hollywood-style movie and, more particularly, in ironing out the exaggerations of Audrey's wide-boned face. On this occasion she used the power of her position to request a change. Renoir took this with good grace, and was replaced by Charles Lang Jr.

Her initial qualms at the news that she was to co-star with William Holden turned out to be

more than justified. Bill's emotional problems, already in evidence during the making of *Sabrina* nine years previously, had rocketed out of control. He was drinking heavily, a tendency that grew worse when he knew he was going to be reunited with Audrey, for whom he still nursed an unrequited love. Throughout the making of the picture his behaviour was highly erratic.

Quine took a house next door to Holden on the Avenue Foch in order to keep an eye on him. However, he was able to exert little control over a man who went on nightly drinking binges, from which he returned to sit by the fishpond gazing at the candles he had lit and floated on the water. Holden also developed the disturbing habit of hanging from the gates of his house like an orang-utan, emitting beast-like howls. After work one evening, wanting to say goodnight to Audrey, he began climbing the outside wall to her second-floor dressing room, ignoring the protestations of Quine and Axelrod. Hearing the yells, Audrey came to the window, and added her voice to the pleas. Holden took no notice, continuing his ascent until he reached her, kissed her on the cheek, and promptly lost his grip and fell. Landing on the roof of a car below, he was fortunate to escape relatively unscathed.

Needless to say, Holden's state of mind was not helpful to his performance, and much time was lost in retakes. Audrey remained loyally supportive and sweet-natured to him throughout, but the toll on her was heavy.

In addition to the on-set problems, she had received news that the Burgenstock chalet had been burgled. Among the possessions of which she had been stripped was her Oscar statuette. (It was recovered in the nearby woods some time later.) Sean and Gina were with her in Paris and, in her state of anxiety, she again began to worry about kidnappers. She dealt with the problem by moving to a rented château outside Paris, owned by the Bourbons and heavily guarded.

Mel was in Madrid completing exteriors for *The Fall of the Roman Empire*. According to biographer Ian Woodward, rumours reached Audrey that he was being seen with a Spanish duchess, precipitating the Ferrers' first major marital crisis. Audrey, apparently, asked for a divorce, which brought Mel rushing to Paris where a reconciliation was effected. Mel joined Marlene

As Gabrielle Simpson in *Paris When It Sizzles*.

Left: With Noël Coward (centre) and William Holden at the Boulogne studios in Paris during the filming of *Paris When It Sizzles*.

Left: One of many zany (some might say insane) moments with William Holden in the movie.

Enjoying a joke with director Richard Quine (left) and Bill Holden.

Dietrich and Tony Curtis in making a cameo appearance in Audrey's movie.

The source material for *Paris When It Sizzles* was *La Fête à Henriette*, a French film of some charm but little distinction, which had been directed by Julien Duvivier in 1952. The premise of the plot promised a pleasant diversion: Richard Benson (Holden) is struggling with a script for a famous producer (Noël Coward), who is furious at the screenwriter's delay in completing it. With two days left to get the job done, the panic-stricken Benson enlists the aid of his secretary Gabrielle (Hepburn), and

the pair act out various possible scenarios. This allows the film to veer wildly between periods and genres in a series of fantasy sequences while — no surprise to the audience — Richard and Gabrielle fall in love.

Audrey wore an array of Givenchy clothes with her usual panache, and the Technicolor looked gorgeous, but this was insufficient to rescue a film that, in the event, suffered from a leaden script. Release was delayed until 1964, when the film received a heavy dose of critical opprobrium. Stanley Kauffman considered that 'the new script embalms the original instead of reviving it';

Hollis Alpert of the *Saturday Review* thought the writing 'fatuous'. But the *New York Times* observed that 'Miss Hepburn, sylph-like as ever, seems slightly bewildered by the trumped-up zaniness in which she is involved', and Judith Crist thought Audrey 'as always, very lovely to look at and so is Paris'. She added, 'Mr Holden, however, is not Cary Grant, even though he tries and tries and tries.'

By that time, however, Audrey had at long last worked with the one and only Cary Grant, and it was her good fortune that this film was released before *Paris When It Sizzles*.

At long last, the magic pairing: Audrey with Cary Grant in Stanley Donen's *Charade*.

It was the director of *Funny Face*, Stanley Donen, who finally achieved the magic pairing of Grant and Hepburn. Donen, an admirer of Hitchcock, had long been seeking a 'Hitchcockian' subject in the sophisticated vein of *North by Northwest*. He finally came upon a short story by Marc Behn and Peter Stone, which, scripted by Stone, became *Charade*, a high-octane, high-definition romantic comedy-thriller.

The complicated plot, with its intricate denouement, centres on the plight of Regina (Reggie) Lampert, the glamorous American wife of a wealthy businessman. While away on a skiing trip with a girlfriend and the friend's small son, she decides to divorce Charles, only to find, on her return, that she is now a widow. Her husband has been murdered and their grand Paris apartment stripped. She is summoned to the American

Embassy by Hamilton Bartholomew (Walter Matthau), who convinces her that it is her duty to help the US government find Charles's missing money, even though her life is being threatened by a richly characterised trio of vicious villains (James Coburn, George Kennedy, Ned Glass) in search of the quarter of a million dollars for which they murdered Charles Lampert, to which they are 'entitled', and which they

Terrorised in *Charade* by, *left*, George Kennedy and, *below*, James Coburn.

paranoia, violence, chaos and romance are heightened through comic contrast, thus eliciting more gasps, they are inverted and raised by the comedy to a grotesque and absurd surreality that makes for a good deal of giggles.'

Charade not only exemplifies this definition, but does so with great stylishness – not just in Audrey's glorious Givenchy wardrobe, but in the camera composition, cutting, and choice of locations. The script sparkles with scintillating repartee. From the zingy titles, and the opening shot of Audrey in glamorous ski-clothes and huge sunglasses, eating with gusto on a snow-capped terrace, her concentration arrested only by a pistol coming into view, Donen's expert control of the visuals and the pace never falters.

Audrey's insouciance and sense of humour are a successful match for Grant's easy expertise, and the age difference is handled with high camp and some skill on the part of both writer and actors. Grant was almost fifty-nine years old at the time; Audrey was thirty-two. But, quite aside from the fact that the grey-haired Grant was still fit and very attractive, the screenplay openly and good-naturedly exploits the age gap. Audrey invites the romance, Cary attempts to keep her at bay with references to his mature years. The

believe is now in the possession of his widow.

Reggie turns for help to Peter Joshua (Grant), a handsome divorcee whom she met on the ski slopes. It is not long before he is seen to be in cahoots with the gangsters, and Reggie learns that his name is not Peter Joshua, but Alexander Dyle . . . Several murders and several changes of alias for Cary later, the truth about him is revealed and the

mystery of Charles Lampert's ill-gotten gains solved. By then, needless to say, the two glamorous leads are going to live happily ever after.

A brief synopsis fails to do justice to a film that is a superb example of its then fashionable genre – a genre of which Joseph Andrew Casper, in his book on Donen, accurately writes, 'While the thriller elements of adventure, suspense and mystery, fear and

Reggie Lampert 'enjoys' a nervous dinner *en bateau*.

Left to right: Grant, Hepburn and villains Coburn and Ned Glass play dumb with Paris police chief Jacques Marin.

verbal cut-and-thrust between them is a delight.

The film is imaginative in characterisation. Audrey's Reggie is subject to compulsive hunger whenever she is nervous, a source of much fun in the film while at the same time always a pointer to a situation of menace.

Once again, the location was Paris. Filming began in October 1962, almost immediately after Audrey had finished her ill-fated outing with Holden. This time it was a happy shoot. The only problem was the weather. Paris was in the grip of an unseasonably cold autumn, which preceded a freezing cold winter. Although this does not show on the screen, it made the location shooting a test of endurance.

Released in December 1963, with a theme song by Henry Mancini and Johnny Mercer soon to be Oscar-nominated, *Charade* was enthusiastically received. *Variety* found it 'seldom falters', Bosley Crowther thought it a 'fast-moving, urbane entertainment' and the leads 'glib, polished and nonchalant'. Pauline Kael considered it the best American film of the year. Thirty years later, the film has lost none of its charm, and can regularly be enjoyed on television. At the time it was a massive box-office hit, which must have delighted Audrey

whose contract with Universal Pictures, who produced it, gave her a percentage of the profits. Cary Grant's comment: 'All I want for Christmas is another movie with Audrey Hepburn.' Ironically, he might soon have been granted that wish, had he not had the wisdom to refuse the offer.

Alan Jay Lerner and Frederick Loewe's musical *My Fair Lady* was not only the multi-award-winning hit of the West End and Broadway in the mid-1950s, but one of the most acclaimed and internationally successful musicals of all time. Adapted from George Bernard Shaw's *Pygmalion*, it tells the story of a renowned English phoneticist, upper-class and a

confirmed bachelor who, for a bet, turns a cockney guttersnipe into a 'lady'. It crowned Rex Harrison's distinguished career, and made a stage star out of a young English rose with a soprano singing voice, Julie Andrews.

After attending the Broadway opening in 1956, Jack Warner, the last of the old-style moguls remaining in a declining studio system, began the long process of acquiring the film rights for his company. By late 1962, having paid a massive $5.5 million for the rights alone, he was ready to proceed. Announcing that he would personally produce the picture, the seventy-year-old Warner signed George Cukor to direct, at a fee of $300,000.

Rex Harrison, and Audrey in her poor flower-seller gear, are instructed by director George Cukor on the set of *My Fair Lady*.

The sixty-two-year-old Cukor, a native New Yorker, had begun his professional life in the Broadway theatre before going to Hollywood in 1929. He worked his way up from dialogue director to co-director, and made his solo début with *Tarnished Lady* (1931), starring Tallulah Bankhead. She was the first of a string of glittering leading ladies, from Garbo, Katharine Hepburn and Norma Shearer to Elizabeth Taylor, Sophia Loren and Marilyn Monroe, who benefited from Cukor's methods and helped promote his reputation as Hollywood's premier director of women. Cultivated, and discreetly homosexual, he also had a volatile temper, and periodically fell out with people. (Halfway through *Gone with the Wind* he was replaced by Victor Fleming, to the great distress of Vivien Leigh.)

Cukor made many fine films on a wide range of subjects. Among his credits were *David Copperfield* (1935), *Camille* (1937), *The Philadelphia Story* (1940), *Born Yesterday* (1950) and *A Star Is Born* (1954). This last, starring Judy Garland in the *tour de force* of her career, was Cukor's only previous musical, but, the musical numbers notwithstanding, it is fundamentally a drama. Of his new assignment he said, 'To me,

My Fair Lady is a play with music . . . If I thought of *My Fair Lady* as a musical, I would not bother with it.'

It was almost a foregone conclusion in the industry that Rex Harrison and Julie Andrews would re-create Professor Henry Higgins and Eliza Doolittle on the screen, but Warner had other ideas. He felt that fifty-five-year-old Rex Harrison was both too old and insufficient a name in movie box-office terms; as far as Miss Andrews was concerned, he adamantly refused even to consider her, since she was a total unknown to cinema audiences. He believed that the insurance of his costly investment lay in Audrey Hepburn, an actress he adored and who had grossed a fortune for his studio with *The Nun's Story*.

An angry and disappointed Alan Jay Lerner could do nothing to persuade Warner otherwise. Meanwhile, the producer approached Cary Grant to play Higgins and James Cagney for the role of Eliza's father, Alfred Doolittle. Both actors refused, with Grant expressing in no uncertain terms his belief that Harrison was the only man for the job. Lerner and Cukor, however, were after Peter O'Toole, who had just completed *Lawrence of Arabia*. Although the film was not yet

released, the movie industry was buzzing with rumours of a new mega-star. Warner went along with this until O'Toole's manager made financial demands that left the mogul gasping. The wheel turned full circle and a relieved Rex Harrison was hired at a fee of $200,000.

Audrey, enjoying a much-needed rest and pleasurable domesticity with her son in the Burgenstock, was blissfully unaware of the machinations going on in Hollywood. In early May, when Mel was at Cannes, hoping to do deals at the film festival, and her mother was staying with her in Switzerland, she received a call from her agent, Kurt Frings, in Hollywood. Not only, he told her, had she landed the plum role of Eliza, for which she had longed, but he had negotiated a fee of $1 million. Only Elizabeth Taylor, for the recently completed *Cleopatra*, had ever received such an astronomical sum.

Stunned and delighted, Audrey called Mel in Cannes. He cut short his trip and came home to celebrate with his wife. By mid-May, the Ferrers, their son (now aged three) and Gina were all in Hollywood. They rented a peaceful and luxurious white villa, complete with pool and tennis court in Bel-Air, and Audrey got down to the very serious business

Covent Garden
Market: 'Wouldn't It Be
Luverly'.

Eliza wants to learn to speak like a lady. Higgins has much to say as his housekeeper (Mona Washbourne) and Colonel Pickering (Wilfrid Hyde-White) look on.

of being coached in a cockney accent and taking singing lessons. The vocal demands of *My Fair Lady*, with numbers such as 'Wouldn't It Be Luverly', 'The Rain in Spain', 'Just You Wait Henry Higgins', the taxing 'Without You' and, of course, 'I Could Have Danced All Night', were a far cry from 'Moon River' and, in *Funny Face*, 'How Long Has This Been Going On?' but she was determined to do her own singing. However, she was not unaware that her ability was held in doubt. At the outset she tackled Cukor and Lerner on this issue. They hedged, and she carried on learning, practising, recording and re-recording.

Shock waves had reverberated through Hollywood when Warner had announced his casting. On this occasion, it was felt that the Hepburn magic was not what was called for. Then, too, the discrepancy between her salary and that of her co-star gave rise to talk. Julie Andrews's biographer, Robert Windeler, however, wrote, 'Miss Hepburn was held in high repute by most of Hollywood, and so after the initial shock of the announcement, talk about it in the industry was short-lived.'

Audrey, none the less, was conscious of the hostility. As Rex Harrison recalled in his autobiography, 'Audrey also had

to weather a great deal of adverse press publicity about how much she was being paid, for most of the press had sided with Julie . . . Audrey is a very sensitive person, and could not fail to feel all this.' The first of many nightmares to come was a press conference hosted by Jack Warner at the Burbank studios on 4 June. With more than a hundred representatives of the world's media present, it was the kind of occasion Audrey had come to dread. Matters were not made any pleasanter when a row broke out between an aggressive photographer and the notoriously sharp-tongued George Cukor.

Doolittle (Stanley Holloway) gets the rough edge of his daughter's tongue at the Higgins establishment.

Eliza loses her poise at the races.

Far left: Audrey in her 'Miss Doolittle' Ascot clothes, with the man who designed them, Cecil Beaton.

Left: Cukor rehearses Audrey's famous ball-gown entrance.

By then, cast and crew were complete. Stanley Holloway was to repeat his memorable stage Doolittle, Wilfrid Hyde-White was to play Colonel Pickering, Gladys Cooper Mrs Higgins, and Mona Washbourne Higgins's housekeeper. Jeremy Brett (who had played Natasha's brother in *War and Peace*) was cast as the lovesick Freddie Eynsford-Hill, who sings 'On the Street Where You Live', and Theodore Bikel was given the striking cameo role of Zoltan Karpathy, the supposed phonetics expert who provides the yardstick of Higgins's success in transforming Eliza's speech patterns.

The British Harry Stradling, a master of colour cinematography, was to photograph the film on the sound stages at Burbank. Although locations had been

Above: Audrey with Assam, on the bicycle Billy Wilder gave her. Beaton took the picture.

Right: Eliza does not wish to be bathed.

Far right: By George, she's *got* it! 'The Rain in Spain'.

scouted in London for scenes such as the Covent Garden exteriors, Warner had later ruled these out on the grounds of cost. André Previn was the musical director and, most significantly from Audrey's point of view, the great English photographer and designer Cecil Beaton, who had designed the stage show, was hired for the film.

The preparation period was more gruelling than any Audrey had so far encountered. She worked a twelve-hour day for two and a half months, singing, taking her dialogue coaching, rehearsing her dance numbers with Hermes Pan, and working with Beaton and the wardrobe and make-up to perfect her appearance. The hairstyles proved particularly difficult, but even more of a problem was the effort to make her look convincing as the grimy street-corner flower-seller of the film's early sequences. They dirtied her clothes, they matted her hair, they forced grime under her fingernails. She hated it. An anecdote has it that she applied unusually generous doses of perfume to herself whenever so dressed.

Principal photography commenced in August, with Cukor

shooting in sequence to assist Audrey in the gradual transition from ugly duckling to swan. At Audrey's request work was carried out on a closed set, with only Mel, and her close friends Givenchy and Doris Brynner allowed in as visitors. With her nerves stretched to breaking point, Audrey couldn't bear anybody to be in her eyeline during a take. Blacks were hung, behind which the crew, with some difficulty, had to crouch. The atmosphere was not improved by the strained relationship between Beaton, an elegant English dandy, reputedly anti-Semitic, and the rough-tongued Jewish-born Cukor. There was an unstated rivalry between them for possession of Audrey, and matters came to a head when, while Beaton was photographing Audrey one day, the director ordered him off the set.

The fissures in Audrey's marriage were now becoming a matter of public knowledge. Although she continued to put a good face on her relationship with her husband, and seemed still to be dependent on him, they were overheard quarrelling in her dressing room. With all the attendant stresses, it was a bitter blow when, after months of hard work and with all her songs recorded, she was finally told that she would, after all, have to be

almost entirely dubbed. To add insult to injury, an underling was despatched to break the news. For the first and last time in her professional life Audrey, distraught, walked off the set. When she returned, it was with a gracious apology.

As André Previn wrote later, '*My Fair Lady* had a very long and difficult music schedule. One of the problems was that Audrey Hepburn could not do her own singing. She was certainly the most beautiful creature imaginable and a lovely actress, but her singing voice, especially when subjected to the mercilessly clear speakers of CinemaScope, was unacceptable . . . Therefore, Marni Nixon, a highly talented and experienced voice double, was hired and put to work.'

Audrey lost eight pounds in weight, and Cukor and Warner became worried about her health. At much financial cost to the production, she was given a couple of days off to sleep. Yet, throughout all these terrible difficulties, she kept her personal unhappiness to herself and retained the outward dignity and grace for which she was renowned. She eschewed the trappings of grandeur consonant with her position as a million-dollar star, riding the bicycle given her so many years before by Billy

Wilder. She also bought and presented Rex Harrison with a similar vehicle.

In his autobiography, Harrison wrote, 'I'd done the show for so long in the theatre with Julie that *any* new leading lady was going to be a problem . . . before we even get to the problem of Audrey's singing, poor Audrey had the unveiable task of taking over Julie's part through no fault of her own . . .' None the less, after some initial wariness on both sides, Rex and Audrey got along well. He wrote, 'Actually, I think that in the end, Audrey gave an enchanting performance on film, and there's no doubt that she contributed greatly to the film's enormous success and lasting popularity.'

On 22 November 1963, during the filming of a large crowd scene, Cukor was given news that President Kennedy had been assassinated. The stricken director found himself unable to speak to the assembled company. An equally shocked Audrey came to the rescue. Grabbing a hand-microphone and controlling her own evident emotion, she said, 'The President of the United States is dead. Shall we have two minutes of silence to pray or do whatever you feel is appropriate.' After the silence, she added, 'May he rest in peace.' Efforts then to

Above: Arriving at Ascot the real lady.

Below: Eliza charms and deceives the 'expert', Zoltan Karpathy (Theodore Bikel).

Overleaf: Rehearsing with Jeremy Brett and Cukor.

Left: Eliza takes her leave of Higgins . . .

. . . and, *below*, comes face to face with her past.

continue with the filming proved futile, and work was suspended for the rest of the day.

By the time *My Fair Lady* opened in October 1964, it had cost Jack Warner $17 million to bring to the screen. It recouped its costs and made a profit of $12 million (and more since). The film effectively marked the swan-song of the traditional Hollywood musical, a genre that gave way to a more modern, youthful and less lavish form.

The story itself and the brilliant score and lyrics have proved timeless and indestructible. Rex Harrison's Higgins transcends his own stage original. The sets and costumes are lavish, the supporting roles well taken, and there is much enjoyment to be had from the film. The exterior scenes, however, are uncomfortably 'stagy' and unconvincing, and the 'fair lady' herself succeeds in only half of her performance.

For all her hard work, Audrey fails to transform herself into a credible street cockney. With the best will in the world, one has to concede that it is a monumental piece of miscasting. However, as she blossoms into a 'lady', the opposite judgement applies. The old Hepburn magic begins to work, and the ugly duckling becomes a swan of rare beauty. From her launch into high society

at Ascot, in which scene her sense of humour serves her well, through to the pathos of her response to Higgins's disregard, Audrey's Eliza weaves a spell. Descending the staircase to be taken to the ball – the exquisite dress is a genuine antique that Beaton found for her – she imprints one of the screen's immortal images of female radiance. No matter that, as London critic Clive Hirschhorn put it, '. . . by no stretch of the imagination would her idiosyncratic speech rhythms have fooled Zoltan Karpathy for an instant.' The entire ball sequence is memorable. One comes away from the film tending to remember the second half.

No reservations were expressed by the American critics when the film premièred at New York's Criterion Theater on 21 October 1964. *Variety* delivered an out-and-out rave, while Bosley Crowther, in the *New York Times*, thought the film 'superlative'. In his view, 'The happiest single thing about it is that Audrey Hepburn superbly justifies the decision of Jack Warner, to get her to play the title role that Julie Andrews so charmingly and popularly originated . . .' He also found her 'almost unbearably poignant in the later scenes when she hungers for love'.

Even more poignant from the star's point of view was the announcement of the Oscar nominations at the end of that year: *My Fair Lady* received twelve nominations (it went on to win in eight of the categories), but Audrey's name was not among them. The final irony occurred at the Oscar ceremony itself. Audrey, exquisite in a white floor-length gown and white gloves, was asked to step in for an ill Patricia Neal, and announce the Best Actor Award. This she consented to do, only to find herself presenting it to Rex Harrison. As if that were not enough, Julie Andrews won the Best Actress Oscar for Disney Studios' *Mary Poppins*, and in a side-swipe at Jack Warner, appreciated by the audience, thanked him for making it possible.

One can only guess at the effort it cost Audrey to weather the snub with her customary charm and grace, under the scrutiny of the television cameras. She did, however, make an uncharacteristic *faux pas* in forgetting to mention Patricia Neal and the reason for her absence (she had had a stroke), an oversight that incurred the wrath of Miss Neal's husband, Roald Dahl.

It was the last word on a million-dollar dream that had turned sour.

Dressed by Givenchy in *How to Steal a Million.*

Personally, I need a lot of loving, being loved and giving love. Love does not terrify me. but the going away of it does

AUDREY HEPBURN

With everything else, Audrey has tremendous guts and strength

GEORGE CUKOR

After completing *My Fair Lady*, Audrey dedicated herself to repairing the cracks in her relationship with Mel. It was contrary to her temperament and her ideals to admit defeat; she still believed that the secret of a successful marriage lay in giving it one's full attention. Despite their difficulties, she and Mel still cared for each other.

Mel had several filming commitments in various European countries. Ignoring the fact that she badly needed rest, Audrey accompanied him everywhere for the better part of a year. The first of a couple of Spanish trips involved Mel in the production of a low-budget film that was being made on location in small and primitive villages. Audrey found herself in conditions of severe discomfort where facilities were few and the food was poor. Nevertheless, she set about helping in whatever way she could, scrubbing, cleaning, cooking and lending a hand on set. Charles Higham describes how 'she had to rise at dawn and stand under a boiling sun all day long with food or production notes like any script girl, and at night she was so tired she often fell into bed without dinner. *She seemed to be acting out a programme of her own making* [my italics] and the effort was considerably exhausting.'

Sean, now four, was a bright, articulate child, whose first language was Italian. He had already picked up Spanish and some English, and had had short spells in kindergartens in Madrid and Los Angeles. His parents were aware that he would soon need to lead a more settled existence and receive regular schooling. In the Burgenstock that meant attending a German school, something that Audrey, with her war memories, refused to countenance. The Ferrers set about looking for a home elsewhere in Switzerland.

By the end of that year, Audrey had finally bought a house of her own. Situated in the tiny farming village of Tolochenaz-sur-Morges, overlooking Lake Geneva and an easy distance from Lausanne, it was a two-storey eighteenth-century Vaudois farmhouse, spacious and simple, built of the local beige-pink stone, and surrounded by orchards. Called 'La Paisible' (The Peaceful), it was just that – the perfect place for Audrey's needs, her European sensibility and her taste for comfort and elegance without opulence. It was to remain her preferred home for the rest of her life.

Sean settled in at the local school a few minutes' walk away, where, being now in French-speaking Switzerland, he added another language to his precocious linguistic accomplishments. Audrey set about the redecoration and furnishing of 'La Paisible'. She relished taking possession of the packing cases filled with treasured objects that had for so long been packed and unpacked in hotel rooms and rented houses. She also began cultivating the garden, which was to flourish and bring her much pleasure. White flowers were her favourites, and her brother sent white tulip bulbs from Holland. Givenchy gave her sixty Iceberg rose trees.

The release of *My Fair Lady* in October 1964 had involved Audrey in a gruelling series of press conferences to coincide with premières in ten cities throughout the USA, as well as in Paris, Brussels, Rome, Madrid and London. Throughout, she dispensed charm and graciousness to all who came into her orbit, and uncomplainingly attended the endless receptions. These included a charity jamboree in France at which President de Gaulle was present, and a lavish party at Cecil Beaton's London home, where Princess Margaret and Lord Snowdon were among the guests.

Audrey was accompanied by Mel on these occasions and, despite rumbles and rumours, they continued to present a united front as a happily married couple, an image cemented by the acquisition of 'La Paisible'. However, a crucial upheaval, which dented their efforts, occurred in Audrey's life at about this time. For several years Henry Rogers, an expert publicist, had been Audrey's personal press and public relations person. They had become good friends and, sympathetic to her needs and temperament, he had served her extremely well. According to Ian Woodward, however, 'Rogers constantly found himself performing a balancing act between appeasing Mel's insatiable desire for Audrey to receive a blaze of publicity on the one hand, and succumbing to Audrey's reluctance to give interviews or pose for photographs on the other.'

Matters came to a head over two specific issues. Givenchy had launched his first perfume, L'Interdit, which was widely advertised in the world's fashion magazines beneath a picture of Audrey, claiming to have been created for her. Audrey, of course, had willingly given her permission for this. Mel was angered by the fact that she received neither a fee nor a supply of the expensive fragrance from the House of Givenchy, a point of view with which his wife disagreed. Rogers, however, acting without Audrey's

knowledge, took the matter up in Paris with Givenchy's brother and business manager, Claude, who was perfectly agreeable to organising some sort of financial arrangement. When Rogers arrived in Switzerland for a meeting with the Ferrers and reported on this, Audrey was outraged at his action.

At this same meeting, it emerged that the director of the Cannes Film Festival had invited Audrey to attend the official opening ceremony. Rogers had responded by suggesting the Festival institute a special award to be given to an individual who had made an outstanding contribution to the film industry, and that Audrey should be the first recipient. It was implicit that Audrey's attendance would be conditional on the adoption of this idea. Favre Le Bret, the Cannes director, took offence and informed Audrey that he felt he was being blackmailed by Rogers.

These two events led Audrey to break off her professional association with Rogers. It was a difficult and distressing decision for her, and one that certain commentators hold responsible for her lack of an Oscar nomination for *Fair Lady*, since it resulted in her not having anyone to undertake the customary lobbying on her behalf. However, she felt

that her publicist had overstepped the mark and breached her trust, leaving her angry and embarrassed. What seems clear is that Rogers, albeit acting independently, had taken his cue from Mel Ferrer, thus emphasising the growing differences between Mel and Audrey. Typically, Audrey did not allow the severance of her professional relationship with Rogers to affect their friendship.

She returned to work in July 1965. Paris was once again the venue, but this time Mel stayed at home in Tolochenaz with Sean. She did, however, fly home every weekend, even if she had only a day to spare. She had been tempted back to work by the offer of a third film with William Wyler, a comedy called *Venus Rising* which, by the time it was released, had changed its title to *How to Steal a Million*.

It is a thoroughly frivolous piece, a slight diversion, which charms and amuses. A caper movie of the *Topkapi* variety, a popular genre at the time, it centres on a heist, as ingenious as it is incredible, and brought Audrey a new leading man, this time three years her junior, the beguilingly handsome and talented Peter O'Toole.

There are faint echoes of *Sabrina* and *Love in the Afternoon*

A most unlikely scrub-woman, with Peter O'Toole and the 'Cellini Venus' in *How to Steal a Million*.

in the casting of Audrey as Nicole Bonnet, the beautiful daughter of a loving widower father (Hugh Griffith). Bonnet *père*, following in the footsteps of his father and grandfather, is a master art forger who, ignoring the pleas of his daughter to go straight, does a roaring trade in 'rare' works. His most prized possession is a small marble sculpture, the 'Cellini Venus', which, to Nicole's horror, he lends to a museum as the centrepiece of a major exhibition.

When Nicole learns that her father is about to be unmasked by the visit of an expert to verify the Venus, she decides to steal it. She enlists the help of Simon Dermott (O'Toole), whom she mistakenly believes to be a professional thief. His plans for the heist involve the pair in having to spend hours in a tiny broom cupboard where, predictably, their romance blossoms (and where Audrey and Peter did a lot of disruptive giggling); and Nicole in having to

masquerade as a cleaning woman. Audrey, in shapeless clothes, down on her hands and knees with a bucket, is the high point of the movie's absurdity – she looks gorgeous. The ploy allows some repartee characteristic of the script: when Nicole asks Simon why she has to wear the clothes, he replies, 'Well, for one thing, it gives Givenchy a night off.'

Alexander Trauner was responsible for building the museum, and for providing dozens

A zany Audrey fools about.

Nicole Bonnet and
Simon Dermott
(O'Toole): partners in
crime.

Gigglers both,
Hepburn and O'Toole
enjoy a joke on set.

of fake masterpieces. They were so impressive that Darryl F. Zanuck (the film was made for Twentieth Century-Fox) organised a showing in Paris and subsequently at Parke-Bernet in New York, all of which was extensively covered in *Life* magazine.

Hepburn and O'Toole make a wonderfully attractive and romantic duo, with Audrey particularly fetching in what was aptly described by Bosley Crowther as 'a gaily eccentric wardrobe of Givenchy costumes'. Crowther thought that 'the whole thing is clearly preposterous – as preposterous as the complicated scheme Mr O'Toole works out for the burglary' but that it is a 'wholly ingratiating film that should leave everyone who sees it feeling kindlier about deceit'. *Variety*, too, gave it the thumbs-up, but there were other critics – particularly in Britain – who were less enthusiastic and for all its charm it was not the hit

that Audrey needed after an eighteen-month absence from the screen.

The Ferrers' efforts to cement their marriage seemed to increase in direct ratio to the seeds of its imminent collapse. That summer they were completing the building of a villa on the Spanish coast at Marbella; later in the year Audrey, to her delight, fell pregnant, but miscarried yet again. There was also a major professional disappointment. Mel had, for

years, wanted to make a movie of
Peter Pan starring his wife, an
enthusiasm she shared. Finally,
legal problems with the rights put
paid to the plan once and for all.
She turned down a million-dollar
offer to co-star in the musical
version of *Goodbye Mr Chips*, but
accepted an offer from Stanley
Donen, which would take her to
France to co-star with the virile,
charismatic and gifted British
actor Albert Finney, seven years
her junior.

The novelist and screenwriter
Frederic Raphael was a skilled
chronicler of the middle-class
morals and manners of the
'Swinging Sixties'. Donen
approached him for a collaboration
and the result was *Two for the
Road*. Set entirely in rural France
and on the Riviera, the story
follows the adventures and
misadventures of Mark and Joanna
Wallace, through a series of road
trips from first romantic meeting
to near-collapsing marriage.

They meet when he is a
penniless young architect, intent
on avoiding commitment, and she
is a virgin, touring with a girls'
choir. Their initially carefree love
affair leads to marriage and a
child, but the marriage is corroded
by Mark's ambition, which brings
success and wealth but also
disillusion, neglect and adultery.

The plot is simple enough, but

The Ferrers with
Assam. Not too
happy.

A little older . . .

Left: Young, poor and in love. Audrey and Albert Finney in *Two for the Road*.

the structure is not. Mark and Joanna's relationship, well described by Joseph Casper as 'a *pas de deux* on wheels', is charted through complex shifts back and forth in time across five different stages which cover twelve years. It is a complicated contrivance – at times very effective, but at others, although handled skilfully by

. . . and then disillusion sets in.

Donen, serving to do little more than confuse.

The theme of the film is serious and there are moments of poignancy and raw pain. The seriousness is leavened by wit, humour and even near-slapstick, which make the piece easily enjoyable, but also undercut its weightier intentions. Also, Raphael's screenplay is periodically marred by a relentless trendiness, a self-conscious bid to to be 'fashionable'.

Two for the Road marked a watershed in Audrey's life and career. If *The Nun's Story* was the most imposing of her films and the first challenge to her ambition to be a 'real' actress, *Two for the Road* gave her her most adult and difficult role. At thirty-seven, she ages backwards with remarkable conviction (and no hint of coyness or easy trickery) to become a girl of no more than eighteen or twenty. She handles Joanna's development with subtlety and incisive control, striking exactly the right note across a broad range of emotional moods. Finney is a well-chosen partner for her, and they both have the back-up of some quality support, Donen's flair, seductive locations and an insinuating Mancini score. In the end, however, the film's beguiling quality rests in Audrey's achievement.

Discussing a scene for *Two for the Road* with Stanley Donen.

There were initial difficulties to be overcome. For the first time in her career, she had to play uninhibited, no-clothes bed scenes; she also had to appear in bathing suits, for which her bony figure was not, in screen-idol terms, ideal. She had to overcome deep self-consciousness of her self-perceived defects. Then, too, Donen was adamant that there was to be no Givenchy. Nervous of the significant, albeit necessary, change of image that the film was to bring for her, this caused her some distress. However, freed of the constraints of the 'hautest' of *haute couture* by the then fashionable, off-the-peg clothes of Ken Scott, Michèle Rosier, Paco Rabanne, Mary Quant, Foale and Tuffin and others, she exhibits an uninhibited physicality that is immensely attractive.

The film also has her playing the clown, capitalising on her

Unaware of lurking
menace, blind
housewife Susy
Hendrix finds her way
home in *Wait until
Dark*.

sense of fun and her generally
underused comic gifts. Always a
great giggler, with a penchant for
making jokes and funny faces, she
found a soul-mate in Finney. They
adored each other, often causing
havoc on set as they dissolved into
helpless laughter. They spent
much time together off the set,
giving rise to inevitable gossip
which did nothing to pour oil on
the troubled waters of the Ferrer
marriage. Indeed, it is difficult not
to make the connection between
Joanna's on-screen suffering and
the real-life difficulties of her
portrayer. Many who worked with
her on the film commented that,
in life as well as on the screen, a
new Audrey emerged – freer, more
extrovert, 'one of the gang' –

although there was no mistaking
the underlying sadness.

Frederic Raphael said of her,
'Audrey's capacity to give a
number of variant readings to the
dialogue, even of unimportant
phrases, from which you could
select the most suitable, was
remarkable. She monitored herself,
as a speaker of lines, with singular
accuracy . . . she combined
naturalism with a sort of stylised
reticence to a rare degree.' He also
said, of her finished performance,
'I don't think I have ever seen a
performance more manifestly
worthy of the Oscar, if that
matters, than Audrey's in *Two for
the Road*.'

The Academy didn't agree. The
film, made between May and

October 1966, was released in July 1967 to mixed reviews, and soon became an art-house film in America. Today, it is regarded as a key work of the period, and Audrey Hepburn's most mature achievement.

By January 1967, Audrey was in the USA to star in a film for Warner Brothers, produced by Mel Ferrer. Playwright Frederick Knott's thriller *Wait until Dark* had enjoyed success on Broadway with Lee Remick in the lead role of Susy Hendrix, an attractive and recently married young woman who has lost her sight in an accident and is working hard to overcome her disability. By a chain of accidental circumstances, Susy's commercial photographer husband (played in the film by Efrem Zimbalist Jr) unwittingly ends up in possession of a doll containing heroin. The dealer, Roat (Alan Arkin), for whom it is destined, and two henchmen (Richard Crenna, Jack Weston), lure Susy's husband away and arrive at her Greenwich Village apartment to recover the doll. The action of the play concerns their various intricate

Richard Crenna (right) and Jack Weston dupe Audrey.

ploys, Susy's dawning realisation that none of them is who he says he is, and the climactic scenes when she is terrorised by the psychopathic Roat.

The part of Susy is a plum role for an actress, and Audrey dedicated herself to the task with her usual commitment. Her account of how she set about it is revealing of her approach to all her work. She told Richard Brown that 'the world's champion blind lady' – as a line in the script has it – 'was a part that I was very happy to be given, but it did cause some anxiety . . . because the studio did want me to be blind in some way, and were rather eager to have me either wear dark glasses or have a scar near an eye, which worried me terribly because, as I say, I don't like the technique to show or even to be there.

'I also felt that this would draw attention to the fact that I'm *not* blind . . . so, my *hope* was to do it from the inside out and to *somehow* convince the audience, who knew that, thank God, Audrey Hepburn is not blind; to, for a fleeting moment, create an illusion of blindness. And two marvellous things happened. One was I spent several weeks going every day to the Lighthouse in New York, the institution for the blind. I was blindfolded, and I learnt what it meant technically

to be blind, to go up and down in elevators, to find something you've thrown on the floor, to make a meal.

'But then I had another extraordinary stroke of – of luck, I would say, but it was a *blessing*. I met a young girl who had in fact been blinded . . . and I said, "Do something for me, find your way around this room." And I sat on my chair and just watched her. She had beautiful eyes, dark, shiny eyes. There was no way of knowing that she couldn't see. So you don't *need* the make-up and the dark glasses . . .'

The film was directed by an Englishman, Terence Young, a successful maker of adventure and suspense movies, who had made his name with some James Bond films, including *Dr No* and *From Russia with Love*. Location filming took place in New York in freezing cold weather, interiors were filmed at Warners' in Hollywood. This time, Audrey had to leave Sean behind in Switzerland to continue his schooling, but phoned and wrote constantly.

She and Mel rented a luxurious bungalow at the Beverly Hills Hotel, with a complete staff. Audrey called a press conference, at which she presided over an elegant English tea and told journalists that the rumours about her marriage were just so much

gossip. It was one of her finest performances. Sean visited during his Easter holidays, and she spent every spare moment taking him on enjoyable outings to Disneyland, the aquarium, and other such places.

On the set, filming proceeded well. It was a good-natured company and Young, an admirer of Audrey's and a gentle and considerate director, handled her well. Every afternoon at four o'clock, at Audrey's behest, the company broke for a full English tea, served in Audrey's own beautiful china. She continued to talk uncharacteristically often to the press; she also lost weight to the point of emaciation.

By the summer of 1967 Mel was spending much time in Paris. Rumours were rife, despite the fact that when she was at home in Tolochenaz he came to see her. *Wait until Dark* was released in October 1967 and was a box-office success. *Variety* thought Audrey gave 'a superior performance' and conveyed 'superbly the combination of helplessness and sense acuity sometimes found in the blind'. As the English film essayist David Shipman has written, '*Wait until Dark* really wasn't great shakes, but she, as a blind girl, made it seem so.' The Academy agreed, and she received her fifth and final Best Actress

Oscar nomination for Susy Hendrix.

But by then, her professional standing was the least of her concerns. It was now public knowledge that her marriage to Mel Ferrer was over. The general consensus among Audrey's friends and colleagues was that Mel, for all his positive qualities and care of Audrey, was unable to cope with her fame, wealth and success, particularly as his own career moved increasingly into the doldrums. Whatever the truth of it, Audrey was devastated.

After passing an unhappy winter of 1967-68, Audrey took Sean to Marbella and sought solace in the sun. There she met the dashing Spanish Prince Alfonso de Bourbon-Dampierre, who became her constant escort, but the romance was short-lived.

Mel, in Hollywood, was incensed at the reports that reached him, while Audrey was similarly outraged by the rumours that Mel was leading the life of a bachelor playboy. Clearly, thirteen years of marriage could not so easily be set aside. They were finally divorced in November 1968.

That summer of 1968, an emotionally exhausted Audrey accepted an invitation from

Stalked by the deranged psychopath Roat (Alan Arkin).

Left: Dr and Mrs Andrea Dotti leave the church after their wedding, 18 January 1969.

Opposite: The advertisement that launched Givenchy's first perfume – and caused a disagreement between Audrey and Mel.

about whether she could produce a son and heir. Then, too, there was a ten-year age gap; this time, Audrey, who would turn forty at her next birthday, was the older of the two.

In due course, all the hurdles were either ignored or overcome. Socially, Audrey's credentials were impeccable, and her irresistible charm and warmth won over the Dotti family. Their romance was conducted with discretion until her divorce was finalised. They spent Christmas with the Dotti family in Rome and announced their engagement. Andrea gave Audrey a magnificent diamond solitaire ring. The problem of a Church wedding was solved by the decision to have a civil wedding in Switzerland.

On 18 January 1969, a pale but ravishing Audrey, wearing a pink Givenchy jersey suit and carrying a small posy, married Dr Andrea Dotti in the town hall at Morges, near Tolochenaz. She was attended by her two closest friends, Doris Brynner and French actress Capucine.

Once again, she resolved to dedicate herself to putting her marriage first. She would not, she said, make a film unless it was on her doorstep; separation was too dangerous for a relationship. She made good the vow – Audrey Hepburn's legion of fans had to wait nine years for her return.

millionaire Paul Weiller and his wife, Princess Olympia Torlonia, to join a cruise to the Greek islands. Among the guests was a handsome, charming, aristocratic and intellectually sparkling Italian psychiatrist, Dr Andrea Dotti. By the time the cruise was over, she had been totally swept off her feet. There were problems: Dotti was a Roman Catholic, she was about to become a divorcee; she was worried about the effect a stepfather might have on Sean; Andrea's family were worried about scandal and concerned

Once she was the only woman in the world allowed to wear this perfume. L'Interdit. Created by Givenchy for Audrey Hepburn.

In Ethiopia in her capacity as roving ambassador for UNICEF.

I have been given the privilege to speak for those children who can't speak for themselves . . . To save a life is a blessing. To save a million children is a God-given opportunity

AUDREY HEPBURN

Audrey Hepburn was in life the exquisite person she represented on the screen. Audrey gave you her heart as if to make you forget her great looks. That rare combination of beauty and success is, I think, what endeared her to the whole world

LESLIE CARON

Audrey Hepburn's marriage to Dr Andrea Dotti was not destined to bring her the happiness she desperately sought. This was not for want of her trying. If anything, she redoubled the efforts to succeed as a wife that had characterised her marriage to Mel Ferrer.

Initially, her new incarnation as a fashionable Roman wife appeared to suit her well. Friends, and the press, commented on a new extroversion in her personality. She seemed relaxed, unworried and outgoing, enjoying the hectic social life that went with her new position. The woman who hated parties was seen to dance the night away; she and her husband frequented restaurants and cinemas, strolling hand-in-hand in the streets. There were happy outings to the exclusive Gambrino Beach Club, where Sean, too, loved to go.

The Dottis had taken a large, spacious and typically Roman apartment on the top floor of a building overlooking the Tiber. Here, Audrey cooked, kept house and interested herself in her professionally distinguished husband's work.

She had long wanted another child. Now, for Dotti and his family, it was a point of honour that she should have one. She was pregnant by the spring of 1969.

Her delight and relief were tempered by the knowledge that childbirth was not easy for her and that, at forty-one, she could ill afford another miscarriage. She decided to spend a long lying-in period at Tolochenaz, far from the bustle of Rome. Already there had been hints that her husband had been seen with other women. During her absence that summer these escalated into gossip-column items, complete with photographs. When he was seen escorting the famous model Daniela, an international beauty with a penchant for courting scandal, the newspapers had a field day.

Andrea flew to Switzerland to see his wife most weekends. What effect the gossip had on her, and on their relationship, can only be imagined, but a shadow of sadness was cast over the general rejoicing when their son Luca was born, by Caesarean section, at Lausanne on 8 February 1970.

Sean was happy to have a baby

Audrey, a young-looking forty-one, with baby Luca.

brother, Dotti delighted to have produced a son. Audrey poured her love into her two children and, when she returned to Rome, concentrated her formidable energies, determination, organisational abilities and exquisite good taste on turning her home into a haven for her family. Sean was sent to school at the French Lycée in Rome; Audrey would cook lunch for her husband each day, and sometimes visit him at the university where she took an interest in all the details of his cases and his research. Andrea calmed down and Daniela disappeared from his life.

When the summer heat grew intolerable, Audrey sent the baby Luca to Tolochenaz to be looked after by his grandmother, the Baroness. She and Andrea visited at weekends and spent August there. This proved helpful to their relationship with Ella, who had not approved of her daughter's hasty second marriage. Audrey's relations with Mel, now living in California, were cool but civil; Sean spent some of his vacations with his father.

During the first five years of marriage to Andrea Audrey was constantly at his side, enduring the Roman summers when he had to work, holidaying with him on the Riviera, travelling to New York and Los Angeles – not as a

film star, but to attend medical conferences as the wife of an important delegate. Although her friendship with Givenchy was as strong as ever, she no longer flew off to Paris to replenish her wardrobe, but frequented the Roman boutiques.

Offers continued to come in for Audrey Hepburn, only to be refused by Mrs Andrea Dotti. She was tempted by *Nicholas and Alexandra*, but left Janet Suzman to benefit from her refusal to go on location far from home; she agreed to star in *The Survivors* for Terence Young on condition the film was shot entirely in Rome, but the project collapsed, as did *Jackpot*, a film about gambling, also for Young; she yielded the comedy *Forty Carats* to Liv Ullmann because it was to be made in the USA. (Ironically, a few years later, she was offered *A Bridge Too Far*, about the Allied disaster at Arnhem, and lost out to Ullmann again – this time because her price was $750,000 against the Swedish star's $150,000.)

In 1971 Audrey consented to appear on a television special for UNICEF, the United Nations Children's Fund, thus sowing the first seed of what was to become her second career. Still idolised by the Japanese, and herself fascinated by their country, she

made a set of television commercials (in Rome) for a Tokyo wig company. Throughout her second marriage, she agreed to periodic interviews for selected newspapers and magazines, continuing to present to the world an image of a perfect life and perfect happiness. She was seldom out of the public eye – anything she did was news, from attending and speaking at the special banquets and awards ceremonies honouring past colleagues to simply walking in the streets of Europe with her children.

Asked by Richard Brown in his 1990 special TV interview whether fame had brought a burdensome downside, she replied that it had brought only its fair share of problems, as with anything else in life.

'The only time it was a little hard for me,' she said, 'was when my second son was born, and I was at that time living in Rome and I could take him *nowhere* – not to a park, not down the street, not put him on a terrace without *paparazzi*. And that was very difficult because, there again, it wasn't *me*, it was bothering the child, you know. Which really drove me mad . . . to have photographers jump out from behind trees and he'd be howling because he was so startled, and *that* was very difficult. But then again, a dear friend who has a beautiful garden in Rome told me, "Bring your child here, with other children, as often as you want." So, again, I was very lucky.'

By 1975 the fashion in movies had changed somewhat from that in Audrey Hepburn's golden years as a star. In general, innocent fun and fairy-tale romance were out, violence, four-letter words and a rasping contemporaneity were in. Audrey, at forty-six, though looking beautiful and younger than her years, was no longer a wide-eyed gamine but a mature woman. The star system, too, had changed. The era of the male-dominated box office had commenced; there was no female star occupying the position that Audrey and her nearest rivals had held in the 1960s. All these circumstances meant that there were few appropriate vehicles to tempt Audrey back to the screen.

That changed when she was sent *Robin and Marian*, an original screenplay by James Goldman. The story rests on an imaginative conceit that brings Robin Hood back to Sherwood Forest, ageing and disillusioned, after twenty years away at the Crusades with King Richard. During his absence Maid Marian has become Mother Jennet, the somewhat unconventional Abbess of a nearby ramshackle convent,

Caught unawares in Rome with Andrea.

which she must defend against religious persecution by King John. Robin and his straggling band of Merrie Men set up camp in the forest once more, and he seeks out Marian. Their former youthful love is rekindled in a spirit of nostalgic regret for time and opportunities wasted until, at the end, with Robin mortally

wounded, Marian poisons him and herself.

Audrey liked the story: 'I think it's a beautifully written script and, after being offered so many films in which I would play the roles I used to play, it was exciting to have a chance to play a woman of my own age.'

The film was to star Sean

Connery – as James Bond, the idol of Sean and Luca – and would be made on location in Spain under the direction of Richard Lester. The supporting cast was of the highest order of British actors – among them Nicol Williamson, Robert Shaw, Richard Harris and Denholm Elliott – and the cinematography in the hands of the superlative David Watkin. The portents were good.

Audrey travelled to Pamplona with her hairdresser Grazia de Rossi, an excited Luca, and the boy's nanny. She found that much had changed in nine years. What remained the same was that, as so often in the past, she had to surmount many difficulties that were not of her making. Richard Lester, an American who based himself in England, was a product of television. During the early 1960s he made commercials and comedies in Britain, working with off-the-wall comedians such as Spike Milligan and Peter Sellers. He came to prominence with the Beatles films *A Hard Day's Night* and *Help!*, as well as those archetypally 'sixties' films *The Knack*, *How I Won the War* and the screen version of the John Antrobus-Spike Milligan play, *The Bed Sitting Room*.

The rest of Lester's *œuvre* was, and is, uneven – often coarse, seldom of interest. Writing in 1991, Max Loppert said that 'as a whole the career seems a classic example of a sizeable and singular talent that simply failed to develop'. He also observed that *Robin and Marian* was 'an unexpectedly graceful piece of cinematic nostalgia' that can be 'accounted an exception to that general rule'.

That most critics responded well to the film is a tribute to Audrey's determination to preserve what she could of those elements that had attracted her to the project. It proved a constant battle. Once at work, Lester was drawn to the male-dominated action aspects of the picture at the expense of the elegiac romance at its centre. He continually whittled away at that: Audrey later said, 'With all these men I was the one who had to defend the romance in the picture. *Somebody* had to take care of Marian.' She had to fight her corner from an unfamiliar position – Lester was not one to bother with 'star' treatment, and no attempt was made to give Audrey the reverent attention she had received in the past. Matters were made more difficult by the director's filming technique, which was to put speed before care.

With her usual tact Audrey later commented, 'I've never made a film so fast, and yes, I'd like to have had more time. But he is very different, extraordinary and spontaneous. Everything has to be *now*, practically impromptu.' Her difficulties can be gauged by a much-reported remark by one of the producers: 'Audrey could get along with Hitler, but Lester is not in her scrapbook of unforgettable characters.'

She had also to battle with being underweight, drinking beer in an effort to combat the problem. This was of little avail, particularly as she was struck down with dysentery and had to cope with uncomfortably changeable weather. She was reclusive after hours, and flew to Rome every weekend to be with Andrea and Sean.

Her playing of Marian displays a depth of understanding of the role, conveyed with warmth, humour, and yearning sadness. She looks undeniably strained – dark shadows are visible under her eyes – but very lovely; the Hepburn of yesterday, just beginning to age. Her performance was warmly welcomed by the majority of critics, although not all of them considered the film a worthy vehicle for her talents. Even the outspoken John Simon, in an otherwise excoriating analysis of the film, concluded, '. . . can you ask for more than Audrey Hepburn and Sean Connery?'

Robin and Marian: the grizzled hero (Sean Connery) and ageing heroine, together again.

Vincent Canby of the *New York Times*, endorsing Audrey's own instincts, thought the film 'ultimately is most appealing as a story of mismatched lovers who found too little too late . . . a hybrid movie, one that seems embarrassed by its feelings; yet it works best when it admits those feelings, when it plays them straight.' Of its stars, Canby wrote, 'Neither Miss Hepburn nor Mr Connery is actually ready for a geriatric ward yet, but their screen presences – the intensity of the images they project – are such that we are convinced that their late August love is important and final, something that I'm not sure Mr Lester knows how to cope with.'

'Mother Jennet', an unconventional abbess.

As pharmaceutical heiress Elizabeth Roffe in *Bloodline.*

Enjoying Ben Gazzara,
one of her co-stars in
Bloodline.

Robin and Marian, for all its
shortcomings, was the last vehicle
that was in any measure worthy
of Hepburn's gifts. Early in 1976,
she went to Hollywood for the
American Film Institute's
presentation of the Life
Achievement Award to William
Wyler. She read a long and

humorous poem of her own, and
was rapturously received. Then,
very nervous as to what kind of
reception she could expect, she
flew to New York for the première
of *Robin and Marian* at Radio
City Music Hall. Her arrival was
greeted by several thousand
cheering fans, chanting, 'We love
you, Audrey.' She was patently
astonished and visibly moved to
the point of tears. Then it was
back to the West Coast for the
opening of the film there, and,
escorted by her husband,
attendance at the Oscar ceremony
on 29 March, where she had been
invited to present the Best Picture
Award. (The winner was *One Flew
over the Cuckoo's Nest*.)

Public acclaim, however, could
not assuage private unhappiness.
Dotti's alleged infidelities and
playboy routine had resurfaced,
with one report in particular, in
the infamous *National Enquirer*,
putting the boot in, and quoting
one of the *paparazzi* as saying that
Dotti was 'a son of a bitch, but
Audrey is a saint'. To Audrey's
sadness was added increased
anxiety about her family's safety,
which had been lent fearsome
credibility by an attempt to
kidnap her husband. Miraculously,
the masked perpetrators of the
attempt were unarmed and, in the
ensuing struggle, Dotti escaped.
Audrey's children were despatched

to the safety of Switzerland to continue their schooling. Throughout these wretched years, during which she continued to turn down offers of work and steadfastly to put an outwardly serene face on her domestic situation, she suffered yet another miscarriage.

Then her old friend Terence Young invited her to star as Elizabeth Roffe in Sidney Sheldon's *Bloodline*, an unashamed potboiler with a multinational cast, multiple locations and a plot generously seasoned with sex and violence. Everything, in fact, that went against Audrey's grain, not to mention that the character in the novel is twenty-three years old. The plot concerns the heiress to a pharmaceutical fortune whose father has been murdered. Taking over the firm, she is threatened by an unknown assassin, with suspicion falling on various members of the family who are vying for power and position. Why did Audrey accept? Nobody really knows.

Terence Young 'spent two weeks persuading her to accept the principle that she might make another movie. The next step was persuading her to read the script. Then persuading her that it was a good script. Then persuading her that she wouldn't wreck her child's life by working again. She's

a very good mother.' On the question of age: 'Is she a girl? No, but she's a consummate actress.'

None the less, even the sublimely youthful Audrey could hardly pass as twenty-three. Sidney Sheldon said, 'If necessary, I'll rewrite the story for the paperback edition. It only needs ten pages to make her a thirty-five-year-old.' And, indeed, that is what the best-selling novelist did.

Audrey was paid $1 million plus a percentage for *Bloodline*. Arrangements were also made to do most of her scenes in Rome, taking her away on location only briefly. She stayed not at home, but at the Grand Hotel, besieged by the world's film journalists, who came from everywhere hungry to interview her.

It was not a happy experience. Actress Beatrice Straight, recalling the location shooting in Sicily, said, 'There was Irene Papas who kept saying she'd forgotten how to act, and James [Mason] muttering he never again wanted to make a film he wasn't also producing and directing, and Audrey who'd come with her own bodyguard, but decided after a while that, on balance, she'd rather be kidnapped by the Mafia than have to complete the picture . . .'

The finished product, released in 1979, again saw Audrey clothed by Givenchy, looking beautiful,

but strained and too thin. British critic Tom Milne summed the film up thus: 'Unutterably chic, inexpressibly absurd, and saved from being painfully tedious only by a personable cast doing their damnedest.'

It had been a trying time. Audrey was in despair over her marriage, and found herself drawn to one of her co-stars, the tough, wiry Italian-American 'Method' actor Ben Gazzara, whose own marriage to actress Janice Rule was disintegrating. Divorce was now in her mind. This was sobering to Dotti and, when filming was over, the couple went to Honolulu for a 'second honeymoon' to try and repair the damage. The differences between them, however, proved too great, and the marriage was effectively over when she accepted a role in Peter Bogdanovich's *They All Laughed*.

Bogdanovich had enjoyed a meteoric rise to fame and success in the early 1970s with two wonderful black-and-white films, *The Last Picture Show* and *Paper Moon*, and the Barbra Streisand-Ryan O'Neal comedy *What's Up Doc?* At forty-one, however, this clever, inventive director, who combined a trendy intellect with a passion for nostalgia, had become better known for his complicated private life than for further

Peter Bogdanovich's unfunny *They All Laughed*. Left to right: Colleen Camp, Blaine Novak, Patti Hansen, Ben Gazzara, Audrey, John Ritter, Dorothy Stratten, George Morfogen. Sean Ferrer is unaccountably missing from the picture.

professional achievements. Audrey was apparently very taken with him, and purported to be taken with the script of *They All Laughed*, which cast her as the unhappy wife of a European tycoon, who, while holidaying in Manhattan with her young son, has a love affair with the private detective hired by her husband to follow her.

That he was played by Ben Gazzara may have influenced her acceptance of a film that is, in every regard, a witless farrago, confused and boring, in which only the sight of Audrey is worth beholding. As Vincent Canby said,

'Any way you look at it – as a comedy, as movie-making, as a financial investment – *They All Laughed* is an immodest disaster. It's aggressive in its ineptitude. It grates on the nerves like a 78 rpm record played at 33 rpm.'

The gossip columnists used their full armoury on Audrey and Gazzara, despite the fact that their brief affair was clearly on the wane, and even hinted, ludicrously, that she was involved with Bogdanovich. In fact, the director was caught up with one of his other cast members, the *Playboy* centre-fold beauty Dorothy Stratten whose jealous

husband murdered her shortly afterwards. Audrey, with her usual loyalty, talked the film up in interviews. Sean, who had finished university and had worked as an assistant on the set of Terence Young's *Inchon*, also assisted on this film and, although without ambitions to become an actor, appeared in it as a handsome, sweet-natured and uncomprehending Spaniard.

While making the film in New York Audrey met the recently widowed husband of the one-time famous screen beauty Merle Oberon. Robert Wolders was tall, strong, bearded and handsome; he

Above: With Robert Wolders.

Below: Ethiopia.

and Audrey began by having their roots in common, for he, like her, was Dutch, and he harboured similar memories – and consequences to his health – of the war years. Wolders, kind, gentle, supportive and uncompetitive, was the antithesis of the men who had usually attracted Audrey. It was a meeting of two similarly bruised souls. The attraction was instant and the bond quickly formed, but the courtship was slow. Audrey was still officially married to Andrea and determined not to jeopardise her custody of Luca; Wolders was still recovering from Merle's death.

By 1981, however, finding strength in their mutual regard, Robert and Audrey began with great discretion to live together at 'La Paisible'. In every way it was the beginning of a new life. The 1980s saw Audrey, who had seemed to spend half her life in an aeroplane, travelling more than ever, sometimes with Robert, sometimes alone. There were several trips to Japan; she attended retrospectives for Givenchy in Tokyo and New York; she flew to London to present the British Academy's Fellowship Award to a deeply touched Fred Zinnemann; she was almost the star of the evening at the American Film Institute's Life Achievement presentation to Gregory Peck. Sad occasions included the funeral of

her old friend David Niven in 1983, and, in 1984, the illness and death of her mother.

Audrey and Andrea were divorced in 1983, when he wished to remarry. There were frequent invitations for Audrey to grace public functions, and countless honours continued to be awarded to her. A prominent occasion was her attendance, in October 1987, as guest of honour at a fund-raising for New York's Museum of Modern Art. In the presence of a wealthy and distinguished crowd who had paid a lot of money to see her, clips from her films were shown and tributes delivered. Billy Wilder said, 'Audrey is one of the few aristocrats left in our business;' Gregory Peck opined, 'There has been no one like her in movies before or since. She has an inner glow which can only come from an inner glow!'

Audrey herself said, 'This evening is really for our children, because only the magic of movies can show them one day how we were – our history, our spirit, maybe even our dreams.'

By the time of the next major tribute, at Lincoln Center in April 1988, it was the children of the world who had become her concern – not whether they might enjoy the movies, but how to keep the tragic victims of famine and war from dying. Like several of her show-business colleagues, she had been invited to become a special Goodwill Ambassador for UNICEF for one year, and she had agreed to do so. The brief was to involve her in fund-raising, raising the profile of UNICEF's work, and visiting the stricken places and people designated to benefit from these efforts.

Suddenly, aged – incredibly – almost sixty, Audrey Hepburn found herself travelling even more, virtually around the world. Overflowing with compassion for the suffering she encountered, she visited the Ethiopian desert bringing what small comfort she could.

Being the woman she was, when her year was up, her commitment was such that she decided to continue her UNICEF work. Travelling in conditions that were often physically as well as emotionally painful for her, and racked with distress at what she saw, she pushed herself to the very limits of endurance as she had always done. Her commitment was absolute, her reward the alleviation of suffering among children. She found herself among cultures as disparate as the Vietnamese, the Indians and various African tribes.

More often than not, Audrey was accompanied on her travels by Robert Wolders, without whose

Snapped in Rome with Sean. Audrey is not pleased.

support, she implied, it would not have been possible to carry on. She told Lynn Barber, 'We've done all this together. He's just as passionate about it as I am.' Barber reported that she 'chain-smoked, ragged with exhaustion' and that her 'commitment is

passionate and sincere. She seemed near to tears as she talked about the "heart-rending" . . . and also "heart-warming" sights she had seen.'

In between her extensive journeys for UNICEF, Audrey made one last film appearance. It

Dacca.

Hanoi.

was a cameo role in *Always* (1989) for Steven Spielberg. Clad in white pants and sweater, she played Hap, an angel who guides Richard Dreyfuss through his arrival in heaven and his subsequent invisible return to earth. It is not, alas, a very successful movie, but Audrey Hepburn, ageing and luminously lovely, could not have been given a better valedictory moment to display the exceptional serenity and sweetness that set her above her contemporaries.

At last, it seemed, she had found contentment. Her children had grown up strong and successful, her private life in the peace of Tolochenaz was truly peaceful, shared with a man who was, finally, the right companion for her. She continued to be in the public eye, revered, adored, imitated – and listened to in a cause that touched her heart and gave a deep purpose to her life. Lost to the film industry, she had transcended its ephemeral fame to become an international figure of wider substance.

HRH Princess Anne, the president of BAFTA, presents her with a British Academy Special Award in London, 22 March 1992.

God has a most beautiful new angel now, that will know just what to do in heaven

ELIZABETH TAYLOR

Audrey Hepburn's
coffin is carried from
the chapel. At the
back, on the right, is
a silver-haired
Givenchy.

Tributes.

Journalists throughout the world composed their obituaries as their final valentines. There has seldom been such a glowing, nostalgic and loving response to the death of a film star. Janet Maslin in the *New York Times* wrote that Audrey was 'the embodiment of grace, generosity and kindness, a performer who filled the screen with entrancing light. With her passing the cinema lost more than a well-loved actress: it lost a swan', and talked of her 'lost, incomparable glamor'.

Anthony Lane felt 'she heightened the spirits of those around her, or made them behave with uncontrollable gallantry. When Audrey Hepburn walked into the movies all heaven broke loose.' Philip French noted that 'beneath the playfulness was an intelligence and a sense of destiny' and, recalling her angel in *Always*, wrote, 'The main consolation the picture offers is that our first close encounter after death will be with an angelic Audrey Hepburn at her most radiant. Dante never made it look so inviting.'

David Shipman observed, 'Many people had expected her to age badly because she had been so scrawny as a young woman. The reverse was the case – for she still possessed in middle age what she had always had: radiance, dignity and, above all, style.'

Martha Sherrill of the *International Herald Tribune* perhaps got to the heart of the matter: 'This gamine-turned-legend transcended fad and the phoniness of her profession, and the seediness. She never seemed to be trying, or wanting. She existed – and what you saw on the screen always seemed to be only Audrey Hepburn, simply existing, but, you know? That was enough.'

The tributes from her colleagues, many of them devoted friends, were equally eloquent. Gregory Peck was 'deeply shocked and distressed'; Roger Moore, another star-turned-UNICEF-worker, declared that 'she was that rare thing in Hollywood – a star who genuinely cared about others before herself.' Her friend and fellow UNICEF ambassador Sophia Loren called her a 'great beauty who enriched the lives of millions,' while to Ronald Reagan she was 'a legend, a true great who will be greatly missed'. George Peppard said, simply, 'A silver bell has been silenced.'

Audrey Hepburn was buried in the cemetery at Tolochenaz-sur-Morges on 24 January 1993. Her coffin was borne by her sons Sean and Luca, Robert Wolders, her brother Ian, her second husband Dr Andrea Dotti, and her lifelong friend Hubert de Givenchy.

It was a small, simple and private ceremony, conducted by the now eighty-three-year-old Pastor Endiguer, who had married Audrey and Mel Ferrer and christened Luca. The Dutch airline tycoon Martin Schroeder brought a bouquet of white 'Audrey Hepburn' tulips, a variety that had been named after her. Those present included Alain Delon, Roger Moore, Doris Brynner, Prince Sadruddin Aga Khan, executives of UNICEF, and a noticeably grief-stricken Mel Ferrer.

Sean Ferrer, speaking at the funeral, said, 'Mother believed in love, that it could heal, fix, mend and make everything all right in the end.' Her last thoughts before she slipped peacefully away, he told the mourners, were for the suffering children of Somalia.

Among the profusion of beautiful floral tributes nestled a simple bouquet which bore the inscription 'From all the world's children.'

This perhaps summed up, as much as anything could, one aspect of a remarkable person, who had lived a remarkable life.

The famous jewellery store – made more so by Audrey's Holly Golightly – placed this tribute in the *New York Times.*

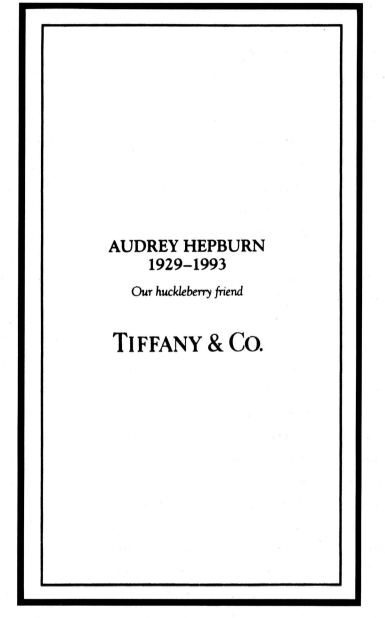

**AUDREY HEPBURN
1929–1993**

Our huckleberry friend

TIFFANY & CO.

FEATURE FILMS

1951 **Laughter in Paradise** (bit part)
Director: Mario Zampi (Associated British)
One Wild Oat (bit part)
Director: Charles Saunders (Eros-Coronet)
The Lavender Hill Mob (bit part)
Director: Charles Crichton (Ealing)
Young Wives' Tale (Eve Lester)
Director: Henry Cass (Associated British)

1952 **Secret People** (Nora)
Director: Thorold Dickinson (Ealing)

1953 **Monte Carlo Baby**
Director: Jean Boyer/Jean Jarrold (Ventura/Filmakers)
Roman Holiday (Princess Anne)
Director: William Wyler (Paramount)

1954 **Sabrina**/UK: **Sabrina Fair** (Sabrina Fairchild)
Director: Billy Wilder (Paramount)

1956 **War and Peace** (Natasha)
Director: King Vidor (Ponti-De Laurentiis/Paramount)

1957 **Funny Face** (Jo Stockton)
Director: Stanley Donen (Paramount)
Love in the Afternoon (Ariane Chavasse)
Director: Billy Wilder (Allied Artists)

1959 **Green Mansions** (Rima)
Director: Mel Ferrer (MGM)
The Nun's Story (Gabrielle Van Der Mal/Sister Luke)
Director: Fred Zinnemann (Warner Brothers)

1960 **The Unforgiven** (Rachel Zachary)
Director: John Huston (United Artists)

1961 **Breakfast at Tiffany's** (Holly Golightly)
Director: Blake Edwards (Paramount)

1962 **The Children's Hour**/UK: **The Loudest Whisper** (Karen Wright)
Director: William Wyler (Mirisch/United Artists)

1963 **Charade** (Regina 'Reggie' Lampert)
Director: Stanley Donen (Universal)

1964 **Paris When It Sizzles** (made in 1962) (Gabrielle Simpson)
Director: Richard Quine (Paramount)
My Fair Lady (Eliza Doolittle)
Director: George Cukor (Warner Brothers)

1966 **How to Steal a Million** (Nicole Bonnet)
Director: William Wyler (Twentieth Century-Fox)

1967 **Two for the Road** (Joanna Wallace)
Director: Stanley Donen (Twentieth Century-Fox)

Wait until Dark (Susy Hendrix)
Director: Terence Young (Warner Brothers)

1976 **Robin and Marian** (Maid Marian)
Director: Richard Lester (Columbia)

1979 **Bloodline** (Elizabeth Roffe)
Director: Terence Young (Paramount)

1981 **They All Laughed** (Angela Niotes)
Director: Peter Bogdanovich (Moon)

1989 **Always** (cameo: the angel Hap)
Director: Steven Spielberg (Universal/United Artists)

INDEX